Mark McGuinness is a wr[...]
people overcome rejection[...]
cess since 1996. He is a co-a[...] [...]-
to-Day: Build Your Routine, Find Your Focus and Sharpen Your
Creative Mind.

Mark's blog at LateralAction.com is read by thousands of people
every week, and he coaches clients all over the world via the magic
of the internet.

*"Achilles' mother dipped him, as an infant, into the waters of the River
Styx to make him invulnerable. Mark McGuinness does the same for
you and me with* Resilience: Facing Down Rejection and Criticism
on the Road to Success. *Read this book and you will be bulletproof!*

*"P.S. The chapters on the Black Box and 'How to Fix It Next Time'
are worth the price of admission all by themselves."*

Steven Pressfield, bestselling author of
The War of Art and *Turning Pro*

RESILIENCE

Facing down rejection and criticism on the road to success

ISBN: 978-0-9575664-0-8

Cover design and typography: IreneHoffman.com

Published by Lateral Action Books
Ebook edition 2012
Print edition 2013

LateralAction.com

resilience

FACING DOWN REJECTION & CRITICISM ON THE ROAD TO SUCCESS

BY MARK MCGUINNESS

LATERAL ACTION BOOKS

Contents

CRITICISM

SUCCESS

NOW WHAT?

INTRODUCTION

INTRODUCTION

Learn to succeed
in spite of adversity

This book will teach you practical ways to develop the **resilience** you need to face down rejection and criticism and succeed in your chosen path.

When you set out to achieve something original and worthwhile with your life, sooner or later you will have to deal with rejection and criticism.

Maybe you're an artist, putting your vision out there for the world to see.

Maybe you're a performer, baring your soul on the stage, night after night.

Maybe you're an entrepreneur, exposing yourself to the verdict of the market.

Maybe you're a sports player, in a brutally competitive arena.

Maybe you're an employee, striving to achieve great things in your career.

Maybe you're a campaigner for change, in the face of inertia and hostility.

Whichever path you're on, there will be two constants:

1. You will apply for opportunities and be rejected, perhaps many times.

2. When you do succeed in getting your work out there in public, you will be criticized—sometimes fairly, sometimes unfairly, and sometimes viciously.

Like most people, you've probably had experiences of procrastinating or shying away from putting yourself forward, out of fear of rejection or criticism. That's only human. But that approach won't get you where you want to be.

If you're serious about making your dream a reality, at some point you are going to have to expose yourself to rejection and criticism—and find ways to face them down and move forward regardless. You will need to develop **resilience**—the ability to bounce back from failure, disappointment and hostility, and keep going.

This book will teach you how to do just that.

Based on my experience of helping hundreds of people get past rejection and criticism and achieve their goals, it gives you the ideas and actions I've found to be most effective—and least painful—in dealing with them.

Step by step, I'll walk you through the process of understanding the true nature of rejection and criticism, and give you practical things you can do to build your resilience.

I'll also highlight some of the hidden pitfalls of success, so that you avoid them and achieve goals that you find truly worthwhile.

I suggest you start by reading through the entire book, focusing on the first section of each chapter. That will introduce you to all the most important ideas, and give you an idea of the territory you'll be traveling through, the obstacles you'll face, and how you can tackle them.

For some of you, this may be all you need. You'll be happy to take the ideas and run with them, applying them in your own way.

Once you've finished your first read-through, go back to a chapter covering an area where you feel in need of help. Look at the second part of the chapter, which will give you action suggestions for tackling that particular challenge.

You probably don't need to act on every suggestion in the book! But I've included specific practical advice for every stage of the journey, so that if and when you need it, you have it.

Whatever you do, DO SOMETHING with the ideas in this book. Doing nothing, or doing the same old thing, will just get you the same old results.

If you're challenged, stuck, or simply afraid, your best way forward is always to try *something* new and see where it gets you.

14

INTRODUCTION

Why I had to write this book

The idea for this book was staring me in the face for years before I saw it.

Since the mid-nineties, I've been coaching people who have big dreams and want to make them happen. Many of them have been artists or creatives of some kind. Others have been entrepreneurs, or people taking an original approach to a range of careers.

My coaching work grew out of my practice as a psychotherapist—I noticed that a certain proportion of my clientele didn't really need therapy, but they were struggling with the mental and emotional pressures of trying to achieve something original in a world that kept putting obstacles in their path. As a writer and poet myself, I found it easy to relate to these clients, and decided to offer a specialist coaching service for creative professionals.

Fast-forward to 2012, and I am coaching clients all over the world, co-ordinating time zones, and conducting sessions via webcam. I am also teaching a free creative career course, The Creative Pathfinder (lateralaction.com/pathfinder). Delivered via email, over 8,000 students are currently enrolled. It covers a different topic each week, such as creative thinking, time management, networking, marketing, managing money, motivation, and communication skills.

At the end of the 26-week course I ask the students a question:

"Which three lessons have been most helpful?"

The answer surprised me, for the most popular lesson is the one I added to the course last, almost as an afterthought: **Dealing with Rejection and Criticism**.

Not only was it the most popular lesson, but students have sent me messages saying: "You could write a whole book based on this lesson."

When I first saw these replies, I realized two things.

Firstly, over the previous sixteen years of coaching hundreds of clients, rejection and criticism were two of the most common challenges I had helped people with. But I'd never thought of 'rejection and criticism' as a distinct issue; it was just part and parcel of the work we did together.

So when I read the students' answers, it was like the moment in a Magic Eye illusion when the image pops out in front of you, as if from nowhere.

And secondly, it struck me that I could indeed write a book about handling rejection and criticism. I had a lot to say on the subject! For one thing, I'd had to deal with my own share of rejection and criticism, as a self-employed coach, public speaker, and writer. And having spent thousands of hours helping clients with the same challenges, I had noticed common themes and solutions. Things I'd heard from clients over and over again. Things I'd said to clients over and over again.

When you work as a coach or therapist, a kind of 'natural selection' occurs as you gain experience. In the beginning you train in different approaches and experiment with all kinds of techniques. Some of them work really well, others not so much. You want to deliver results for clients, so you stick with the ones that work best, and leave the rest aside. So over time, the techniques, tips, questions, and stories that are most helpful to clients are the ones that survive. They adapt and evolve as you refine them through work with many clients.

When I saw people asking for a book about rejection and criticism, I realized it should be fairly straightforward, and that I could compile all the 'fittest' ideas, stories, and techniques from my own experience and coaching practice. So that's what I've done.

As I wrote, I imagined sitting down with someone and having a conversation one-to-one. Someone with big dreams, and a sense of huge potential inside them. Someone who knows they have to put themselves forward—to be rejected, judged, and criticized—if they are to achieve their goals. Someone who is excited at the prospect of achieving their ambitions—and secretly a little scared inside.

Someone like you.

This book contains the most effective ideas and techniques I've used in my own life, as well as with hundreds of clients, to help you overcome rejection and criticism and achieve something amazing with your life.

Some of the advice in this book has been informed by scientific research, or other people's thinking, but none of it is based on theory. These ideas have been road-tested in my own experience and that of my clients—real solutions for the real challenges you face.

So that's my part of the bargain—I've collected my best advice on handling rejection and criticism en route to success. Your part of the bargain—should you accept it—is to take these ideas and experiment with them, trying new approaches to the challenges you face, to see if they get you closer to your goals.

Do we have a deal?

RESILIENCE

CHAPTER 1

The guardians at the gate

On a mountainside high above the ancient Japanese city of Kyoto stands the Zen temple of Kiyomizu-dera. Founded in AD 772, the huge temple is built entirely of wood, without a single nail.

You approach the main entrance along an avenue of shops selling fans, ceramics, kimonos, and other souvenirs. Near the gate is a fountain for visitors to purify themselves by washing their hands. Water gushes from the jaws of a little metal dragon.

Stone steps rise to an impressive gatehouse, its timbers painted brilliant orange, the roof's lip lifted to show its frilled underside, like a mushroom cap displaying its gills. Staring at the splendor of the temple, it would be easy to walk right up to the gateway without noticing the two guardians who have been watching your approach.

But look either side of the entrance and you will see a green wooden lattice concealing a chamber within, like a sentry booth. Peer through the lattice and you meet the gaze of a demon.

These two statues are called *Nio*, and are traditional guardians of the Buddha. On the left stands Misshaku Kongou Riki-shi, mouthing the syllable 'ah' (equivalent to the Western 'alpha' meaning birth); on the right stands Naraen Kengoou, making the sound 'un' ('omega' meaning death). The gate is open, but to enter the temple you have to walk between them.

According to Zen priest Steve Hagen, the Nio represent Paradox and Confusion, which all spiritual seekers have to overcome in their quest for Truth. The mythographer Joseph Campbell described them as Guardians of the Threshold to Adventure—archetypal spirits who rise up to threaten the hero as soon as he or she dares to step outside her comfort zone and accept the challenge of the quest.

When you set out to achieve something remarkable with your life, your way ahead may look clear and straightforward.

As you first dare to dream, you feel the thrill of adventure. Picturing your goal, you see yourself achieving something original, meaningful, inspiring, fulfilling. You see all the rewards within your reach, and the benefits you will bring to others.

All this is as it should be.

If you're not fired up to achieve your ambitions, you probably haven't found your true calling yet. But this initial excitement is usually followed by a more sober realization. Looking ahead, you start to think of all the obstacles that lie in your way. And the thought occurs to you that before you can realize your ambitions, you'll need to confront two guardians as powerful as the Nio—the twin specters of Rejection and Criticism.

Now logically, neither of these specters can hurt you—they are no more life-threatening than a couple of painted statues. But when you stand naked before them, and feel their eyes piercing your very soul, giving you a foretaste of the pain, humiliation, and despair that rejection and criticism can inflict, then you'll understand why so many have turned back, and abandoned their dreams rather than endure their pitiless gaze.

But those who run away when faced with rejection and criticism do so because they have failed to grasp an important secret about Threshold Guardians. Baleful as they look, their purpose is not to destroy their hero—but to test you, to see if you are ready for the adventure.

Joseph Campbell points out that some Nio statues are carved with one hand held up as a warning, telling you to stop—but the other hand is actually beckoning you forward. *The Guardian's job is to frighten away the immature and unready, but to allow safe passage to the hero with sufficient courage to look them in the eye and keep moving forward.*

If you're serious about facing down rejection and criticism in order to succeed in your chosen path, if you're eager to step over the threshold, this book will show you how.

NOTES

Steve Hagen, *Buddhism Is Not What You Think*, (HarperOne, 2003)

Joseph Campbell, "The Power of Myth," (PBS television interview, 1988)

CHAPTER 2

The bigger the dream,
the bigger the fear

The day I received my provisional license to practice as a therapist, I felt like I'd received my provisional license to pilot the Space Shuttle. My journey had taken me so far beyond my wildest expectations I felt like I was in orbit.

After the practical exam, I floated back to London's Paddington Station on a current of euphoria. Everything was very clear and sharp—the faces of people, newspapers blowing past, adverts for the shows playing in the city on that particular day.

When I got on the train I couldn't contain my excitement. I got up and walked up and down the carriages several times. I felt the energy of the train rushing through the dark countryside, the energy of the stars hurtling through space.

The day I saw my first therapy client was a very different matter.

I found myself in a small consulting room in a health club. There were no windows and it was dark outside anyway. From the other side of the wall, I heard huge crashes and thuds from an aerobics class, presumably for ogres or giant robots. Not exactly ideal conditions for a relaxing hypnotherapy session.

My mouth was dry. I took another sip of water. I was sure I could hear my heart pounding.

The receptionist rang to tell me my client had arrived. Which meant the client was now *between me and the exit.* There was no way out.

What on earth had I done? How could I have been so naive as to think I could do this? All the books I'd read were no help to me now. I was a complete beginner. Why hadn't I waited and trained a bit longer?

But deep down, I knew this was what I wanted. And the fear was just the price. There was no way out, so I might as well face up to it.

I took a deep breath, stepped into the corridor and smiled.

——

It's no coincidence that those were two of the most intense emotional experiences of my professional life. Looking back, it's obvious that one was simply the flipside of the other—the natural consequence of a principle I've repeated to countless clients over the years.

THE BIGGER THE DREAM, THE BIGGER THE FEAR

When you dream a big dream, it will enchant you and sparkle with anticipation. New vistas will open up before you. Promises will beckon you forward.

But—as we've seen, when you first met the gaze of the Threshold Guardians—once the initial rush of excitement has passed, you start to think of all the things that could go horribly wrong. And the fear kicks in.

At this point the Guardian's job is to sift the wheat from the chaff by putting on its most terrifying mask, so that you do one of two things:

1. Run away, with the fear in hot pursuit.
2. Hold your nerve, embrace the fear, and step forward.

Now, the immature and unready want to have the good things without facing up to the fear. They want to order success like a pizza, or download it like a movie—instantly and easily. But success isn't like that.

The bigger the dream, the bigger the fear.

This explains why some people put themselves through unspeakable, terrifying (and unnecessary) ordeals, since they know the flipside of this kind of fear is joy:

- **THE IRONMAN TRIATHLON**—a 2.4-mile swim, followed by a 112-mile bike ride, followed by a marathon 26.2-mile run (with no breaks).
- **WINGSUIT BASE JUMPING**—zooming down a mountainside at over 100mph, inches from the rock face, wearing a flying-squirrel-type suit with wings between the arms and legs. (I'm not joking—put 'wingsuit base jumping' into YouTube and see for yourself.)
- **THIRTY-MAN KUMITE**—a karate test where one fighter takes on 30 fresh opponents, one after the other, in quick succession.
- **KAIHOUGYOU**—a 1,000-day, 40,000-km running challenge undertaken by the 'marathon monks' of Mount Hiei in Japan. Starting in the first year by running 18.5 miles per day for 100 days, the test peaks in the seventh year, with 100 days of 52.5 miles per day.

Even if you have no ambition to be a daredevil, you've probably noticed that the most thrilling experiences in life are usually pretty scary:

- starting a business
- getting married
- having children
- performing on stage

- competing in a tournament
- writing a book

So how can we handle the fear?

TO CONQUER FEAR, ACCEPT THE FEAR

Mother Nature provided us with fear, so let's give her the benefit of the doubt, assume she knew what she was doing, and work with what she gave us.

It's fine to put on a brave face in public, but don't kid yourself. When you set yourself a big challenge, you should *expect* the fear to rise up before you. You should look out for it and even welcome it—because if you don't experience much fear, it's not much of a dream.

Paradoxically, the fear is less intense if you don't resist it. Because you know it's normal, you don't panic. As John Eaton likes to point out, the message of fear is *not* to run away and hide, but to be alert, to face your challenge, and deal with the obstacles you face. When you do that, the fear subsides as naturally as it arose—and your dream is still beckoning you forward.

YOUR NEXT STEPS

1. Think about a big dream you have, or a big challenge you're facing. Picture yourself committing to making it happen. Visualize it as realistically as you can, and tell yourself you're really going to do it… then wait for the fear.

2. When you start to feel the fear in your body, don't resist it or try to ignore it! Stay centered and alert, and observe exactly where

in your body you experience the fear. Breathe into it, and allow yourself to experience the fear, realizing there's no need to panic.

3.   Notice what thoughts are going through your mind. If you catch yourself running a 'mental disaster movie,' switch it off! Imagine taking the disc out of the DVD player and snapping it in two.

Now load a 'mental rehearsal movie'—in which you see yourself dealing effectively with the challenge, surviving and succeeding in your goal.

4.   Stay with the fear until you feel it start to subside naturally.

5.   Do something concrete that will take you one step closer to your goal. Even if it's a small action, notice how it reduces the fear.

NOTES

For insights into the 'endurance mindset' of leaders and endurance athletes, visit Jarie Bolander's site www.enduranceleader.com

For more on Kaihougyou, read *The Marathon Monks of Mount Hiei* by John Stevens (Shambhala, 1988).

For an inspiring story of courage in the karate dojo, read *Waking Dragons* (Summersdale Publishers, 2006), Goran Powell's account of completing the thirty man kumite, fighting thirty opponents one after the other.

For more on how to handle fear and other troublesome emotions, see John Eaton's blog: www.reversethinking.co.uk

CHAPTER 3

Why do rejection and criticism hurt so much?

"Just don't take it so personally."

"Why are you so down? It's not a matter of life or death."

"It's not like it's the end of the world."

"Sticks and stones..."

If anyone has ever said any of these words to you in the wake of a brutal rejection or stinging criticism, you'll know how stupid and feeble they sound—however gently spoken, and however well-meaning the speaker.

When you're hit by rejection or criticism, it shakes you to the core. It feels impossible *not* to take it personally. Logically, it may not be a matter of life and death, or the end of the world, but it sure as hell feels like it. And words most certainly can hurt. Paper dragons breathe real fire.

WHY YOU CAN'T HELP TAKING IT PERSONALLY

When you put your heart and soul into something—whether a work of art, a performance on a stage or sports field, a business, or a job you passionately want to succeed at—then it becomes an extension of yourself. It's not just an object or a game or a business or a job.

The end result is not a 'product' or a 'performance'—it's a part of *you*.

And when you identify with something that is then rejected or torn to shreds by a critic, it's impossible not to take it personally. As the novelist Gustave Flaubert put it more poetically:

> A book is essentially an organic thing, a part of ourselves. We rip a piece of gut from our bellies, and serve it to the bourgeois. Drops of our hearts' blood are visible in the characters of our writing. But once printed, goodnight! It belongs to everyone.

This is why you flinch when the envelope comes through your letterbox, or the email lands in your inbox, or the phone rings and you know you're about to learn your fate.

This is why it hurts when you fail to land that job, or that part, or that contract.

Or when a reviewer trashes your work.

Or when someone you respect damns it with faint praise.

You put everything you have into your work, so any judgment on the work feels like a judgment on you as a person.

But this is a good thing.

Because when you feel rejection and criticism personally, it shows you care about your work and you're pouring yourself into it. If it stopped hurting, it would mean you had stopped caring.

This is true for everyone who is passionate about what they do, no matter how much they achieve or how successful they become. Believe it or not, it's even true of writers of books about dealing with rejection and criticism...

Poetry is my own art form, and for several years, I've been attending Mimi Khalvati's classes at the Poetry School in London. High-quality criticism is my main motivation for doing the class. Not only is Mimi one of the most sensitive and helpful readers of poetry I've ever come across, but the class is full of experienced poets who offer insightful critiques of each other's work. But the thing is, it's usually easier to appreciate the quality of the feedback while we're discussing *other people's* poems.

But when it's *my* poem on the table, it's a different matter.

Now, I've worked with hundreds of artists and creatives on how to deal with feedback and respond to it constructively. I know I shouldn't take it too personally. I should remember that the comments are a judgment on the work, not on me. Obviously. But that doesn't keep my heart out of my mouth when I stop reading and wait for the first response.

And sometimes it doesn't stop that little voice starting up in the back of my head, wondering: *"Why did you read out such a load of crap. No wonder they're sitting there in silence. They're cringing at how bad it is, and wouldn't you?"*

You can probably relate a similar story from your own experience. When assessing other people's performance, you may well have a finely developed sense of judgment. But when it comes to critiquing your own work, it's incredibly hard to look at it with anything like objectivity. It feels too close, too personal, too painful.

OK—now for the good news.

It will—and should—always hurt.

But the sting does get less sharp with time. As we'll see in Chapter 9, repeated exposure to any stimulus—including rejection or criticism—will desensitize you to it. And when you sharpen your own critical thinking skills, which I'll show you how to do, you'll be less likely to take criticism at face value.

YES, IT IS A MATTER OF LIFE AND DEATH

The pain of rejection and criticism isn't confined to taking it personally. It's also accompanied by a sense of dread that—our friends try to reassure us—is way out of proportion to the actual threat posed by a situation such as not making the hockey team, or having a manuscript returned by a publisher.

Or is it?

The psychologist Abraham Maslow famously proposed a hierarchy of human needs, stacked up like a pyramid. The bottom level contains basic **physiological needs** (oxygen, food, sex, sleep), with the next level up **safety needs** (security, employment, shelter). The next two levels are **love and belonging** (friendship, family, sexual partnership) and **esteem** (self-esteem, confidence, respect). Right at the top is **self-actualization**, where we fulfill 'higher' needs such as creativity, morality, personal development, and wisdom.

According to Maslow's original paper, we need to prioritize lower-level needs (survival and safety) before we can move on to higher needs (social interaction and personal development). 'Belonging' is clearly a need that is threatened by rejection, and 'self-esteem' is threatened by criticism. So Maslow's pyramid seems to confirm that rejection and criticism are *not* life-threatening.

Since you're reading this book, the chances are your goal falls into the category of self-actualization: you're not looking for mere survival or acceptance, you want to realize your potential and make a contribution to the world. Now I have a lot of respect for Maslow's work, but if we take his pyramid at face value, this kind of goal can look a bit like a luxury item—something you pursue if you can afford it, once your other needs are being met.

But this doesn't quite add up when you consider all the people who have prioritized self-actualization over 'lower level' needs such as survival or social acceptance. For example, the stereotypical starving artist; or charity/public sector workers who accept a reduced income in pursuit of a cause in which they believe. An extreme example is someone like Gandhi, who put his life on the line many times, including going on hunger strike in protest at violence, demonstrating his willingness to sacrifice his own survival for the greater good. Even if you haven't gone to this extreme,

I'm sure you can think of times when you chose to sacrifice some of your own needs in pursuit of higher principles or ambitions.

Another challenge to Maslow's hierarchy comes from psychological research that suggests we experience social exclusion with the same intensity as a threat to our survival. In *Your Brain at Work*, a superb book about applying the findings of neuroscience to everyday challenges, David Rock highlights the research findings that the same neural networks are used to process both social and survival needs. So whether we feel hungry or cast out from the tribe, we experience the same terrifying sense of threat.

Humans have survived and evolved by collaborating. How else did we outwit the proverbial saber-toothed tiger? We certainly didn't out-muscle, out-run, or out-bite it. But we found safety in numbers, and in our combined ingenuity. So for most of human history, membership of the tribe was a matter of life and death. If you were excluded for any reason, your chances of survival dropped dramatically.

And what is rejection but exclusion from your chosen tribe? If you want to be a sports player, not making this year's team means you're out of the tribe—and you may never get back in. It's the same story if your book manuscript is rejected—it feels like another nail in the coffin of your ambitions to join the tribe of writers. Ditto failing to land a job: excluded from the tribe of [insert name of your desired profession], you start to wonder whether you should go back to waiting tables, sweeping chimneys, or whatever is your personal definition of the job you'd least like to have.

In each of these scenarios, rejection feels like being cast into the outer darkness where there is weeping and grinding of teeth. (And licking of lips by saber-toothed tigers.)

How does this relate to criticism?

Just recall the difference between someone criticizing you in a private conversation versus bawling you out in front of the whole group. Or between receiving a scathing comment about your work in a private email and in a review in the biggest newspaper in the land.

Public criticism can lower your status in the eyes of the tribe. And the people who tell you not to worry about other people's opinion obviously don't know about the research into the effects of social status on monkeys.

Like humans, monkeys organize their society hierarchically —every member of a monkey tribe knows his or her place in the hierarchy, and it's possible for outsiders (human or monkey) to identify an individual monkey's status from its body language.

Researchers have discovered that when a monkey moves up or down the social ladder, this has direct, measurable, physiological effects—including the release of hormones, gene activity, white blood cell count, and the strength of the immune system. Every time a monkey moves down the ladder, its nervous system downgrades itself. And each time its health and vitality is downgraded, its chances of survival shrink a little more.

So each time you are publicly criticized, you feel as though your social status is slipping a notch or two. You may not be out the door yet, but you're one step closer to the exit. One step nearer the outer darkness. Which is why rejection or criticism *feels* like a matter of life or death, however much you try to tell yourself it isn't.

But it doesn't have to feel like that forever. As we'll see, there are plenty of things you can do to lessen the impact of rejection and criticism, and to develop the quality that will keep you going in spite of them: resilience.

NOTES

Mimi Khalvati: www.mimikhalvati.co.uk

The Poetry School: www.poetryschool.com

Gustave Flaubert, letter to Ernest Feydau, 11 January 1859

David Rock, *Your Brain at Work*, Scene 10 "Turning enemies into friends" (HarperCollins, 2009)

Maslow, A.H. (1943). "A Theory of Human Motivation," *Psychological Review* 50(4): 370-96

Sarah Zhang, "Low Social Rank Messes with Monkeys' Immune Systems by Altering Gene Expression," lateralaction.com/monkey-research

CHAPTER 4

Make it something worth dying for

Since rejection and criticism are a matter of life and death, there's no point exposing yourself to them for anything less than a dream worth dying for.

I'm serious.

Whichever path you choose in life, sooner or later you will experience a moment when you feel tested to breaking point. On this day, the obstacles will be stacked so high, the rejection so brutal, the criticism so cutting, the people you encounter so hostile, petty, dishonest, ungrateful, or plain nasty, that you feel stretched to your limit—and beyond. When that day comes, you will slump down in a heap and ask yourself why you bother.

And you'd better have a good answer ready.

Because if you're doing a job or running a business just for the money, it won't be a good enough reason to pick yourself up out of that heap and rise to the challenge.

If you're a dilettante, toying with your talent in the hope of fame, fortune, or the adoration of fans, that won't be enough either.

If you're doing something because it's what's expected of you by your family, friends, or peers, that won't be enough.

If you're doing something because you're good at it, the rewards are easy to obtain, and it feels like the path of least resistance, that certainly won't be enough.

At that point, getting a raise, or a corner office, or maximizing shareholder value, or even a medal, or your name in lights won't be enough.

At that point, it will feel like your identity—your very essence—is on the line. Going forward means risking the loss of your place in the world, your opportunity to live your life to the full and actualizing your potential. It means risking obliteration.

So when you ask yourself why you bother, and whether to risk going on, it will make all the difference in the world if you've chosen a path worth dying for.

Because in that case, your decision will be simple—not easy, but simple.

You will have a reason to take the next step, to risk it all, and to meet the challenge with every ounce of your strength.

You'll be prepared to put yourself on the line, and take whatever flak or pain comes your way. You'll feel a fountain of strength rising up from your core, picking you up, and helping you to endure whatever is coming your way—failure, humiliation, shame, disappointment, hurt, or whatever—and to push beyond it.

So what on earth is worth dying for?

It needs to be something you are passionate about. Here are a few suggestions:

- **JUSTICE**—righting a big wrong.
- **GENEROSITY**—helping others survive, thrive, and achieve all they can be.
- **ACHIEVEMENT**—amazing the world with something spectacular, extending the limits of what's humanly possible.
- **INSPIRATION**—touching people's hearts with the beauty, sorrow, and wonder of life.
- **KNOWLEDGE**—adding to the store of human knowledge, about ourselves and the universe.

- **PROTECTION**—preserving what's most precious, such as people, civilized values, or the environment.
- **JOY**—enjoying life and giving pleasure to others.
- **LEADERSHIP**—taking responsibility and using power for the common good.
- **WISDOM**—understanding what's truly important: how to live a good life.

When you're connected to one or more of these principles, it's like plugging in to a massive power grid, giving you an inexhaustible source of inspiration, motivation, and resilience.

This does not have to be an obviously 'noble' cause, such as saving the world or helping others directly—unless that really is your core passion. Remember the famous Indian saying: better to fail in your own destiny than succeed in someone else's?

MY TWO DREAMS WORTH DYING FOR

When I was a teenager, I fell head-over-heels in love with poetry. When I read or listen to a real poem, I experience a magical, spine-tingling quality that I don't find in any other art form. And when I spend time writing poetry, my whole body feels completely different, as if the words are echoing and resonating all the way down to the tiniest cells.

But most people don't care about poetry. There's no money in it, and precious little fame. And it's fiercely competitive. The vast majority of poems submitted to magazines and publishers are rejected. And even if you manage to achieve some kind of recognition, there will be plenty of people prepared to take you down a peg or two. So each time you write a line of poetry, with the ultimate aim of trying to publish it, you are putting yourself—if you'll excuse the pun—on the line. But I can't imagine giving up on poetry. To misquote Samuel Johnson: "When a man is tired of poetry, he is tired of life."

The other goal worth dying for that I'm pursuing is in my professional life. After experimenting with various career options, I've committed myself to helping creative professionals—artists, creatives, entrepreneurs, and other mavericks—as a coach and trainer. I'm doing this partly for selfish reasons—out of all the types of client I've worked with, they are the most fun, and are inspiring and consistently interesting to spend time with.

Another reason is that we are living at the time of incredible opportunity for creative people, when it has never been easier for them to find inspiration, education, collaborators, and an audience for their work. And (no coincidence) at a time when the world urgently needs creative solutions to the problems we face. I want to help people seize this opportunity.

Now, I'm not curing cancer or saving the planet, so I'll be the first to admit there are plenty of worthier causes than writing poems and helping artists succeed. But I believe everything we do has a ripple effect. The more people who are out there full of enthusiasm and creativity, inspiring others, solving problems, and creating different types of wealth, the more opportunities we have to make the world a better place. So by spreading a little inspiration as I go, I trust that I'm playing my small part.

And like everyone who has worked for themselves, I've experienced the lows as well as the highs of the entrepreneurial rollercoaster. I've experienced financial hardship, frustration, disappointment, loneliness, and all kinds of bad behavior from certain individuals I've encountered along the way. There have been plenty of days when I've asked myself why I bother, and when I have been profoundly grateful to have a good answer ready.

Being connected to my passions means that on most days, I get out of bed full of enthusiasm. I can't wait to get started on my work—writing, coaching, teaching, helping, and connecting with aspiring creative people, online and in person. And even on the worst days, I have a reason to keep moving forward, and put myself on the line for what I believe is important.

I wrote this book because I want you to have that same enthusiasm, that same sense of purpose, that same resilience, on the day when you really need it.

YOUR NEXT STEPS

1. Ask yourself:

- What path are you on at the moment?
- What makes it important to you?
- Does it feel like something worth dying for?
- Is it something you'd be prepared to put yourself on the line for?

If you can answer a definite 'yes' for the last two questions, you can skip the rest of this section. If not, the following steps will help you work out what it is you want to commit yourself to achieving.

2. Which of these principles resonates most strongly for you?

- **JUSTICE**—righting a big wrong.
- **GENEROSITY**—helping others survive, thrive, and achieve all they can be.
- **ACHIEVEMENT**—amazing the world with something spectacular, extending the limits of what's humanly possible.
- **INSPIRATION**—touching people's hearts with the beauty, sorrow, and wonder of life.
- **KNOWLEDGE**—adding to the store of human knowledge, about ourselves and the universe.

- **PROTECTION**—preserving what's most precious, such as people, civilized values, or the environment.
- **JOY**—enjoying life and giving pleasure to others.
- **LEADERSHIP**—taking responsibility and using power for the common good.
- **WISDOM**—understanding what's truly important: how to live a good life.

Now ask yourself:
- Where and when did you feel most strongly connected to this principle?
- What ideas does that memory give you about a path you would feel passionate about following?
- What else could you do to express this principle?

3. Beware of making this decision with your head!

Your body won't lie to you: Read through the list again, slowly, while paying attention to your body. Notice when you feel the strongest emotional response.

Don't worry if you find it hard to sense the emotional signals from your body. I'll introduce you to a method in Chapter 6 that will make this easier.

CHAPTER 5

Why you need to build resilience

The list of people who succeeded at the first attempt and lived happily ever after is very short indeed.

There is a much longer list of people who encountered rejection, criticism, disappointment, failure, and other setbacks, before they gained a modest level of recognition and reward for their efforts. They then encountered *more* setbacks, often way out of proportion to the rewards they reaped.

Have a look at the list of "30 famous authors whose works were rejected repeatedly (and sometimes rudely) by publishers" published by Examiner.com (this link will take you there: later-alaction.com/famous-rejections). The names include Stephen King, William Faulkner, William Golding, John Le Carré, George Orwell, Sylvia Plath, and Marcel Proust. Whatever your field of endeavor, you could probably compile a similar list of superstars who were rejected and humiliated over and over.

Somehow they managed to go on in spite of adversity, to learn from their mistakes, to improve their skills, and persist until they succeeded.

In order to do this, they had to develop a quality that set them apart from the legions of also-rans: **resilience**.

The word 'resilience' comes from Latin: 're' (back) + 'salire' (jump). It means to jump back, spring back, or to bounce back.

Taken literally, it describes the physical properties of an object; it is also frequently used as a metaphor for a psychological ability.

PHYSICAL RESILIENCE

An object has resilience when it can be bent or stretched and then spring back to its original shape, without permanent damage or distortion.

You have probably heard the story of the reed and the oak tree buffeted by a powerful storm. When the storm struck, the oak tree laughed at the reed bending in the wind, and boasted of its own strength. But when the storm intensified, the oak's rigidity was its downfall: it was uprooted by the wind and crashed to the earth. When the storm passed, the oak still lay on the ground, its roots exposed to the air, while the reed sprung effortlessly back upright.

At first glance an oak tree looks much stronger and more impressive than a reed. Yet the reed survived because it possessed *flexibility* **as well as** *strength*—**the combination that produces resilience.**

PSYCHOLOGICAL RESILIENCE

In psychology, the word 'resilience' refers to a person's ability to deal with stress and bounce back from adversity—again, without permanent damage or distortion.

Some psychologists have argued that resilience is a personality trait: you either have it or you don't. But it is more commonly understood as a process, influenced by many different factors, and an ability that can be learned and strengthened. And it is not just confined to individual psychology—our relationships with other people have a big impact on our resilience, positive or negative.

To me, **resilience means the ability to keep pursuing your goals in spite of adversity.** It is driven by passion, the fuel that keeps you going in spite of disappointment, rejection, and criticism. And because it is an *ability*, you can learn it and improve with practice, just like any other skill.

In this book I will teach you practical ways to develop the resilience you need to overcome rejection and criticism. I'll show you how to change your thinking, harness your emotions, and build relationships in order to strengthen your personal resilience.

NOTE

Michelle Kerns, "30 famous authors whose works were rejected repeatedly (and sometimes rudely) by publishers," lateralaction.com/famous-rejections

CHAPTER 6

A simple but powerful way to develop resilience

Fifteen years ago, I attended my first silent meditation retreat.

Each morning we woke at 5am to begin a long day of sitting and walking meditation. We spent an hour a day on 'working meditation,' mostly housework in the retreat center. The rules included no talking (apart from essential practicalities), no phones, no computers, no books or magazines, no sex, no alcohol, and no TV, radio or entertainment of any kind. The last meal of the day was at 10.30 in the morning.

It was a wonderful experience.

Looking back, I can see that what I learned on the retreat has done more than anything to help me build resilience in the face of rejection, criticism, and disappointment. And the most important lessons were the ones right under my nose.

TWENTY MINUTES TO TRANSFORM YOUR LIFE

If this were a book about physical resilience, I'd be recommending a program of exercises to develop your bodily strength and flexibility. But our aim is to develop **psychological resilience**. So we need a different type of exercise.

I should warn you that this exercise is very simple. So simple you may find it hard to see how it could possibly help you. But having used it for fifteen years, as well as recommending it to countless clients and seeing the benefits to them, I'm recommending it to you without reservation.

Here it is: *sit still and do nothing for twenty minutes a day.*

There. I told you it was simple!

Actually there's a little more to it than that.

As you sit, pay attention: to the feel of the chair you are sitting in; to the sensations in your body; to the colors and shapes you see around you; to the sounds you can hear; to your breathing; to your thoughts; to your feelings.

The object of the exercise is NOT to put yourself into a relaxed state of mind. It's simply to pay attention to your experience—physical, mental, emotional—right here, right now.

And that's it.

On the one hand, sitting still for twenty minutes probably sounds too short—you may well be reading this and thinking, "How will twenty minutes of doing nothing help me achieve my dreams?" On the other hand, when you actually try to *do* it, twenty minutes can feel an awfully long time. In no time at all, you feel bored and fidgety. You want to get up and do something more interesting and productive.

So why would you want to do something that seems so feeble, pointless, boring, and difficult? This is one of those things that you really have to experience for yourself to be convinced, but I'll have a go at giving you a taste of what's in store if you try this and stick with it for a few days:

- Your mind becomes clearer, and your feelings become calmer —even though you are NOT consciously trying to relax.
- You start to see your thoughts coming and going, and realize that they are not as real as they seem.

- The same happens to your feelings.
- You notice how easily you can get caught up in unhelpful states of mind—and that it's possible to escape from them.
- You spend less time wrapped up in your thoughts, desires, and fears, and pay more attention to your experience in the present.
- Problems don't seem as big and unsolvable as before.
- Keep practicing and you will start to notice these same benefits in real life, not just during your twenty minutes of practice time. You will feel less anxious, and more present. When good things happen, you will enjoy and appreciate them more. When you are faced with a challenging situation, you won't feel as overwhelmed as before. You will find yourself acting more decisively, authentically, and effectively. It will be easier to have difficult conversations, and more fun to spend time with friends and family. You will feel more alive.

MINDFULNESS

The usual name for this practice of paying attention is **mindfulness**.

If you're spiritually minded, you may like to know this practice is the foundation of just about every mystical tradition, including Buddhism, Sufism, Hinduism, and esoteric Christianity, and has been taught in various forms by teachers including the Buddha, Gurdjieff, Krishnamurti, Aldous Huxley, and Eckhart Tolle. There's no need to adopt a new set of beliefs or find a new teacher; you can add mindfulness to whatever form of prayer or meditation you already practice.

And if you have a more secular outlook, you may like to know that you don't need to subscribe to any religious beliefs or follow any spiritual tradition to experience real, tangible, measurable benefits from mindfulness practice. A growing body of psychological research demonstrates the benefits of mindfulness practice in dealing with anxiety, stress, and pain, as well as strengthening concentration, producing positive emotional states, and even boosting the immune system. An alternative term for mindfulness used by many psychologists is **Attentional Training**, or AT for short.

Mindfulness practice has been applied in many different contexts, including spiritual and personal development, psychotherapy, sport, and learning. It is also the single most powerful thing you can do to develop resilience.

HOW MINDFULNESS BUILDS RESILIENCE

Mindfulness helps you develop the psychological strength and flexibility that combine to produce resilience. This has a paradoxical effect that is hard to describe but pleasantly surprising to experience.

On the one hand you feel much more vividly aware of your thoughts and feelings, but on the other, they don't affect you as much as before. It's as though you are holding them at arm's length, yet without becoming detached from them. And this changes the way you experience both rejection and criticism:

- Rejection and criticism still hurt, but not so much as before.
- They don't feel so overwhelming or so final.
- You don't take them so seriously or so personally.
- You start to see them in perspective—you are more aware of alternative viewpoints and don't take critics' words as the last word.

The benefits of mindfulness practice are enormous, but they don't happen overnight. It's a steady, drip, drip, process. Because of this, it's easy to overlook your progress, or to feel discouraged and give up, or just to skip it, because it feels like it won't make much difference.

But if you stick with mindfulness, you will notice a real change. I'll keep referring to mindfulness throughout the book, assuming that you are practicing it on a daily basis. (I'll also assume you'll give up and re-start several times before you're convinced of its value. I know I did.) And rest assured I will teach you plenty of thinking techniques and action-based assignments to help you tackle specific aspects of rejection and criticism. Mindfulness is like a catalyst—if you practice it, every other technique in this book will become more powerful.

YOUR NEXT STEPS

I can't take the credit for this technique. It is thousands of years old, and has been taught in different variations by many teachers. I learned it as part of my training as a psychotherapist, and also from the monks at Amaravati Buddhist monastery (www.amaravati.org).

1. Decide on a time of your day when it will be impossible to 'forget' to practice, and when there are fewest interruptions and distractions. Most people choose first thing in the morning or last thing at night.

2. Decide where to sit. If you're flexible enough to sit cross-legged on a cushion, that's great. It will help to keep your spine erect and make it hard to doze off. But it's fine to sit in a chair—not a comfy reclining armchair, but one that allows you to sit up straight, with the soles of your feet on the floor.

3.   Decide how long you're going to sit. If in doubt, aim low, and start with five minutes a day. No matter how busy you are, you can spare five minutes, so that's one excuse blitzed. And if you have a low boredom threshold and start fidgeting sooner rather than later, it's easier to start with five minutes than twenty. As you get used to it and feel the benefits, you can gradually extend your practice to twenty or thirty minutes a day.

4.   When it's time to sit, switch off all your phones and put them out of reach. Make sure people around you know you are not to be disturbed.

5.   As you sit, pay attention to your experience in the present:

- Physical sensations.
- What you can see (yes, you can keep your eyes open, or close them if you prefer).
- Sounds you can hear.
- Thoughts that enter your mind.
- Your feelings.

6.   It may help to focus your attention on your breath as it enters and leaves your nostrils. Don't try any special breathing techniques or deep breaths! Just pay attention to your natural breath as it comes and goes.

7.   Inevitably, your mind will wander. You will 'come round' from time to time and realize you have been caught up in all kinds of daydreams, memories, worries, and fantasies. Don't beat yourself up over this! It's normal. The important thing is to notice when it happens, and bring your attention back to the present.

8. Don't let boredom put you off. If you start to feel bored, don't resist it—notice what it's like. What kind of thoughts and feelings is it composed of? Keep your attention in the present, and the boredom will pass. Trust me.

NOTES

For an excellent introduction to mindfulness meditation, see Steve Hagen's *Meditation: Now or Never* (Penguin, 2012).

For an overview of the types and benefits of Attentional Training (AT) as well as how to use it to deal with fear and uncertainty in the pursuit of big dreams, see Chapter 7 of Jonathan Fields' book *Uncertainty: Turning Fear and Doubt into the Fuel for Brilliance* (Portfolio/Penguin 2011).

For another mindfulness technique, and more mindfulness and meditation resources, visit the resource page for this book: lateralaction.com/resilience-resources

REJECTION

REJECTION

Rejection comes first

Rejection is when someone says 'no' to you or your work. You don't get the part, or the job, or the book deal, or the recording or consulting contract, or whatever it was you'd set your heart on.

Traditionally, rejection comes first. You need to persuade a gatekeeper, such as a job interviewer, editor, producer, casting director, or commissioner, that *you* are the one who should be given this opportunity. Only then do you get to do your thing (and expose yourself to public criticism).

These days, the internet gives you options for putting yourself and your work out there in all kinds of ways, without the need to charm a gatekeeper first. So in some contexts, you can bypass rejection (and go straight to criticism!). But there are still plenty of opportunities that require a thumbs-up or thumbs-down from gatekeepers. You don't get to compete in the Olympics or star in a West End show or run for president by starting your own blog.

Sometimes rejection comes hand-in-hand with criticism. But often rejection is made even harder because you *don't* get any feedback. The answer is 'no' but you don't know why.

For our purposes I'm going to separate out rejection and criticism, highlight the different types of challenges they present, and show you what to do about them.

On with the rejection…

REJECTION

CHAPTER 8

It's normal

You know that feeling like a horse just kicked you in the stomach?

The one that hits you when you open the envelope or the email and the first words you see are *"I'm afraid..."*

Or when the voice at the other end of the phone says, *"I'm sorry but..."*

Or when the other person looks you in the eye and clears their throat, and you realize they are not smiling.

It's normal.

And you know how you feel when the news really sinks in that this fabulous opportunity is not going to happen for you?

That feeling when you go home and it feels like your world has fallen in, that you're a failure and you were stupid to even consider putting yourself forward. What were you thinking? How embarrassed they must have been to have to put you out of your misery and confirm that yes, you are a complete and total failure and you'll never amount to anything so why don't you just give up now. And how are you going to face the world and tell them about your latest, biggest, and most spectacular failure?

That's normal too.

And you know how it feels like you're the *only one* locked out on the outside with your failure, while all the gorgeous, talented, lucky, successful, confident people are celebrating on the inside (and laughing at you so hard champagne comes out of their noses).

That's normal too, believe it or not.

I should know.

For one thing, I've experienced all those feelings myself.

But that's not how I know it's normal. If that were all the evidence I had, then it could just be you and me who have felt like that.

But it's not just you and me.

You see, I'm in a privileged position. Over the past sixteen years, I've spent hundreds of hours as a coach and therapist, listening to people in the process of changing their lives and pursuing their dreams.

I've worked with rich people and poor people. People feeling lost and confused over their direction in life, and people on a mission to change the world. People who were just starting out and people with a long list of hits to their name. People struggling to break out of obscurity and people struggling to cope with fame.

The one thing they all had in common was that they were trying to achieve something remarkable with their lives. They were all pursuing a dream.

And you know what? At some point, most of them told me a version of the same thing:

Everyone else looks so confident and sure of themselves, unlike me, with all my doubts and insecurities.

If only I were a bit more like them, I wouldn't keep getting rejected. I'd be a success.

After I'd heard variations on this theme several hundred times, I started to realize it wasn't just me. **It was normal.**

You see, when you set yourself a big ambitious goal, chances are you're chasing an opportunity a lot of other people would like to have:

- A lucrative book or recording deal.
- A well-paid job doing fulfilling work with inspiring people in the coolest part of town.
- The lead role in a play/movie/dance production.
- Funding and advice for your startup from wealthy, experienced, well-connected investors.
- A place in a top sports team.

If it were easy, everyone would be accepted and no-one would ever be disappointed. But it isn't easy.

So most people are disappointed, most of the time.

In other words, it's normal to be rejected and to feel the horse-kick in your stomach.

Everybody gets rejected. Even the best of the best. In fact, the best probably get rejected even more than the rest of us—because they put themselves out there more, take more chances, and pursue more opportunities. As Babe Ruth said: "Never let the fear of striking out get in your way."

Remember the list of 30 famous authors who suffered multiple rejections at the start of their career?

How come *they* were the ones who succeeded, when countless others fell by the wayside?

I think we both know it wasn't just talent, or luck, or privilege. Those are the classic excuses we make when we want to belittle others' achievements, or take pity on ourselves.

In the light of so much evidence of early rejection and later success, it's hard to escape the conclusion that *they kept going in the face of rejection.* They didn't get an easy ride. They weren't led past the queue of rejects to a VIP entrance. They experienced the same pain and fear and anger and embarrassment as you and me. And they accepted it as **normal**. Par for the course. An occupational hazard. Something that goes with the territory. A price they were willing to pay. Even a badge of honor.

They weren't too proud to trudge through the mud in pursuit of their dream. So why should we be?

My clients often have a 'light bulb moment' when I tell them I've heard the same anguish over rejection hundreds of times—even from very successful people. Even though nothing has actually changed about their particular situation, it's clearly a weight off their minds. Once they get this, they stop beating themselves up so much, and telling themselves there must be something wrong with them. And start dealing with the reality of the particular rejection they've just received.

"Someday," I tell them, "I'm going to get you all in a room together, so you can compare notes and see how many people feel the same way!" That might be logistically challenging, so the next best thing is to write this book and get it into the hands of as many readers as I can.

Rejection on its own is hard enough. But rejection plus telling yourself, "It's just *me* who's useless enough to be rejected," is a real killer. So drop the second part. Next time you get rejected for a fabulous opportunity, don't hide from the pain. But don't add to it either. Look the rejection in the eye and see it as a normal stopping point on your journey. Then take your next step.

YOUR NEXT STEPS

1. Read through the list of famous writers whose works were rejected multiple times, and notice whether it changes the way you feel about them. Access the list via this link: lateralaction. com/famous-rejections

2. Now make a list of your top ten heroes—people who achieved amazing things in your own field, and/or people you admire for their achievements in other fields.

3. Read up on their careers—especially the early stages—and look out for stories of rejection and perseverance in the face of adversity. Chances are you'll find plenty.

4. How did they cope with rejection? Look for little clues in the reports of things they said or did. What can you learn from their example?

5. Next time you experience rejection, notice how much of the pain and anxiety comes from the rejection itself—and how much you are adding to it by treating it—and yourself—as abnormal. Then stop adding to it.

REJECTION

CHAPTER 9

Get used to it

I don't mean that in a nasty way, how some people say it: "Life's not fair, get used to it!" I just mean that since rejection is normal, it's something you'll have to get used to.

As we saw in Chapter 3, it's a *good thing* that rejection hurts—it shows you are putting your heart and soul into your work. If it stopped hurting, it would mean you had stopped caring. But over time, the sting does get less sharp. Psychologists call this **desensitization**, and it's the basis of behavioral therapy for phobias. By repeatedly exposing yourself to the source of your fear (spiders, lifts, public speaking, heights etc.), you learn to tolerate it a little better each time.

When I delivered my first client session, it was a scary experience, but sixteen years later, having worked with hundreds of clients, I'm very relaxed about doing another one.

It was the same story with public speaking. When I first did it, I was terrified. I hardly slept the night before a presentation. I would practice for hours for a talk that only lasted a few minutes, and felt a huge relief each time it was over.

But years later, having given hundreds of talks, presentations, seminars, interviews, and podcasts, as well as several best man's speeches, I'm now very comfortable standing and talking in front of an audience. To make me nervous, something new and potentially tricky has to be introduced into the mix—such as a much bigger audience, or a potentially hostile one.

When you first encounter a potentially threatening situation—like trying to spear a stampeding woolly mammoth, or auditioning for a part in a play—your emotional brain is on high alert, pumping you up with the cocktail of chemicals, led by adrenalin, which produces the classic 'fight or flight' response. But the more mammoth hunts and auditions you take part in (and survive), and the better you get at dodging tusks and remembering your lines under pressure, the less fear you experience, because your emotional brain is getting the message that you can handle this kind of thing without a major panic. Familiarity breeds comfort.

The worst thing you can do is shy away from the thing you're afraid of. This keeps it unfamiliar and uncomfortable. It turns it into A Big Deal. It means you have to work yourself up to it each time. And it makes the desensitization process take longer.

So the more mammoth hunts and auditions you go to, the more competitions or trials you enter, the more manuscripts you send out, the more jobs or funding you apply for, the more rejections you'll get, but the less it will hurt each time.

YOUR NEXT STEPS

1. Remember the first time you experienced professional rejection. On a scale of 1–10 (1 = best, 10 = worst), how bad did it feel?

2. Now remember a more recent rejection. On the same scale, how bad did that one feel?

3. If you notice that you feel better about rejections as time goes by, that's a sign that you are acclimatizing to them and treating them as a normal part of the process.

4.   If you notice that rejections tend to feel *worse* as time goes by, read Chapter 12 to see whether you are making things harder for yourself than you really need to.

5.   Make a list of all the opportunities you would be applying for if you weren't afraid of rejection. Now imagine you've applied for all of them—and been rejected by nearly all, but have received one or two acceptances that have made the process worthwhile.

Look at yourself in the future and see that when you reach that stage, you will not be so bothered by each rejection. The sooner you start applying for those opportunities, the sooner you get to feel like that for real.   69

70

REJECTION

CHAPTER 10

Roll with the punches

When I started learning aikido, the first thing we were taught was how to fall and roll. The idea was that until you knew how to receive an attack, you weren't ready to be attacked.

We rolled forwards and backwards, sideways to the left, and sideways to the right. We practiced single rolls and double rolls, rolls in small tight circles, and big loping ones. Sometimes a student held a wooden sword out a few inches from the ground, for us to roll over. (The higher your grade, the higher the sword was raised.) Sometimes a student knelt on the mat and we rolled over him—without touching. Sometimes there were two or three students lined up, and we had to leap over them, Evel Knievel style, landing and rolling on the other side. At that point, technique became very important!

Rolling out of the way of an attack does two things. Firstly, it protects you from the full force of the blow. If you stand and resist it, you are liable to be injured by the blow itself or to be knocked over and injured by the fall. But by accepting the force of the blow and moving with it, you have a much better chance of avoiding injury. Secondly rolling takes you away from the attacker, giving you a split-second to stand and face the next attack.

The same principles apply to rejection. If you try to resist it, by pretending you don't care, it will hit you just as hard—only you won't be prepared.

Remember, *it's supposed to hurt*.

In private, allow yourself to really feel whatever emotions rise up—such as fear, anger, embarrassment, or sadness. Don't try to rationalize them or explain them away. Roll with the punches and trust that you'll come out the other side. And don't keep it to yourself. Talk to someone—a friend, partner, teacher, or mentor—anyone who cares about you, understands your situation, and will listen to you (without trying to 'fix' the situation by offering advice).

Therapist John Eaton likes to point out that if you suppress your emotions, they don't go away—they keep pushing to be released, because they have something important to teach you about your situation. But if you acknowledge the emotion and express it—in words or actions —it fades away, having done its job.

John likes to quote these lines from William Blake's poem 'A Poison Tree':

> I was angry with my foe,
> I told it not, my wrath did grow.
> I was angry with my friend,
> I told my wrath, my wrath did end.

Bottling up your feelings just means you'll end up carrying them around with you in the bottle, which has a tendency to break and release the contents—in the form of a temper tantrum or floods of tears—at the worst possible moment.

I remember reading an interview with one of my sporting heroes, the football (soccer) manager Martin O'Neill, where he said he allows his players 48 hours to celebrate a win or to feel sorry for themselves after a defeat. If the team has won, he doesn't want them getting carried away. And if they have lost, he *wants* to see them sitting disconsolately on the bus home, to see that they care.

Supposing you gave yourself 48 hours after a rejection, to roll with the punch and process the emotions it brings?

During that time you're allowed to take a break, spend time with friends, treat yourself, or have some quiet time alone—whatever it takes to deal with it. If it's a major disappointment, 48 hours won't be enough to recover completely, but it's a good starting point. By disciplining yourself (that's right, it's a discipline) to take a break after each rejection, it will help you recover more quickly and learn more from the experience.

YOUR NEXT STEPS

1.   Next time you're rejected, give yourself 48 hours (or whatever time frame feels right) to roll with the punch.

Give yourself permission to take a complete break, give yourself a treat, spend time with a friend, go for a walk—whatever it takes to give yourself a breathing space and process the experience.

2.   During your daily mindfulness practice (you haven't skipped it already, have you?) pay particular attention to your feelings, and the sensations in your body. What emotions are you experiencing?

3.   Give yourself permission to express your emotions in a safe context e.g. crying, yelling, talking to a friend, or writing an angry letter to the person who rejected you, but whatever you do, don't send it!

4.   Ask yourself: What can I learn from this experience? What will I do differently in future?

5.   When the 48 hours (or however long you've chosen) are up, get back on your feet and back to work.

NOTES

Thank you to Sensei Tony Ecclestone of Meridian Aikido Club for introducing me to aikido. www.meridianaikido.org.uk

John Eaton's blog about the brain, the mind, and personal change: www.reversethinking.co.uk

CHAPTER 11

Wallowing is for pigs

One more thing about rolling with the punches: you don't just roll around on the floor, or lie there in a heap. You have to roll *straight back up again*—into a standing position, ready to defend yourself.

In the *ukemi* part of an aikido grading test (that's the falls and rolls), the moment you stand upright again, two black belts try to push you over—so you need to recover your balance instantly. If you keel over, you fail. (The higher the grade you're testing for, the quicker and harder the black belts push.)

When it comes to rejection, the difference between rolling down and straight back up is the difference between feeling pain and wallowing in it. Developing resilience means not flinching from or avoiding the pain—you need to feel it to learn the lesson. But it also means not adding to it and perpetuating it by going into 'poor me' mode—replaying the rejection over and over in your mind and telling yourself what a terrible injustice you've suffered.

Wallowing is for pigs, not people.

Remember O'Neill's 48-hour limit? When the two days were up, the players had to report for training again and give 100% commitment. So when your time is up, it's time to get back on your feet and take the next step down the road.

YOUR NEXT STEPS

1. Put limits on your recovery time. Forty-eight hours is a good rule of thumb, but work out what works best for you. Whatever you do, don't carry the rejection around with you like a permanent scar.

2. Be honest with yourself. When you're feeling down, ask yourself how much of the bad feeling is pure pain, and how much of it is wallowing? Some clients even find it helps to put a percentage on this: "I was feeling pretty down on Tuesday, but it got easier once I realized it was only 40% genuine pain and 60% wallowing!"

CHAPTER 12

Seven guaranteed ways to make rejection worse

It's easy to say 'Don't wallow,' but not so easy to avoid doing it. When you've just been hit by rejection, a lot of the thoughts you experience are automatic, or semi-conscious. If you're not alert to them, they can make you feel much worse than you need to. So here's a handy field guide to some of the most damaging thoughts you can think in the wake of rejection and what to do about them.

1. TAKING IT PERSONALLY

OK hands up, I said it's natural to identify with your work and take rejection or criticism personally! And so it is. You need to put everything into your work if it is to be any good—so any rejection of your work feels like a rejection of you. And if you get turned down for a job or a place on the team, then in a very real sense it is a rejection of you.

But beware of taking any specific rejection—or even a series of rejections—as a blanket judgment on yourself and your entire career. William Golding's best-selling novel *Lord of the Flies* was reportedly rejected by at least ten publishers before it was finally accepted. Supposing he'd said, "OK, nine rejections prove I'm not a real writer. All those experts can't be wrong. There's no point sending it out again."

Remember, just because you or your work were not the right fit in any particular situation, it does NOT mean you are fundamentally incapable of achieving your ambitions. So watch out for any thoughts that suggest that this is the case!

WHAT NOT TO SAY TO YOURSELF
- "I'm a failure."
- "I'm a loser."
- "I'm not a real artist/writer/footballer/whatever."

WHAT TO SAY INSTEAD

- "I didn't make it this time, but I'm still a good athlete/leader/ chef."
- "I wasn't the right fit for them, but there will be other people who love me and what I do."
- "OK I'm not the world's best right now, but if I keep learning from experiences like this, I can get there in future."
- "Just because I screwed up this time, doesn't mean I can't get it right next time."

2. REPETITION

It's bad enough being rejected once, but you make it much worse for yourself if you keep replaying the experience over and over in your mind. The most depressed people I have ever met were constantly running a 'disaster movie' in their minds, made up of all their most painful rejections and failures.

When you've suffered a rejection, it's an excellent idea to sit down and review your performance, to see what you can improve in the future. But once you've done that, and decided how you're going to improve, it's time to archive the mental movie.

Your mindfulness practice will help you to do this, by focusing on what you can see, hear, feel, touch, taste, and smell in the present.

When you are present, it's easier to stop watching the disaster movie.

WHAT NOT TO DO
Keep playing the mental movie of your rejection(s), complete with a doom-laden voiceover, reminding yourself how bad it was.

WHAT TO DO INSTEAD
i.   Make time to review your performance. Hold yourself to high standards, and be unflinchingly honest. (If you can, get someone who knows you well to help with this.) What can you learn from the experience? What can you do differently next time?

ii. Once you've done this, archive the mental movie:

1. Close your eyes and visualize the DVD player and TV screen you're using to watch it.
2. Then imagine pressing the 'stop' button, taking the DVD out of the machine, putting it back in its place, and then locking it in a secure cabinet.
3. Then return to your comfy armchair, and put on a DVD showing you making positive changes, improving your performance and achieving success in future. (Mental popcorn is optional—fortunately it's very low-calorie!).

iii. Once you've done the review, and archived the movie, put it out of your mind. Use mindfulness to stay in the present and let go of it.

3. REGRET

This one goes hand-in-hand with repetition. Not content with reminding yourself what an awful experience it was, you also torture yourself by thinking it could have turned out so much better—if only you'd done this or that differently. So you beat yourself up for having been so 'stupid.'

What you're forgetting here is the fact that hindsight is always 20:20. If you had known then what you know now, then of course you would have done things differently!

But you didn't, so you didn't. And even if you had, there's no guarantee it would have brought you success.

So bin regret.

It's not doing you any favors. Instead, focus on what you can start doing now to bring yourself success in future.

WHAT NOT TO SAY TO YOURSELF
- "If only I'd done X, I wouldn't be so miserable."
- "What if I'd done X? Just imagine how happy I'd be now."
- "I'm so stupid. I should have done X."
- "Why on earth did I do that? What was I thinking of?"
- "I really messed up my chance; I'll never get another one like that."

WHAT TO SAY INSTEAD
- "I did the best I could at the time. I'll do better next time."
- "Hindsight is 20:20. The most important thing is to learn from it."

4. PREDICTION

This one's a real killer. It's where you tell yourself that, because you've been rejected in the past, you will always be rejected in the future. Which is completely illogical, but frighteningly persuasive!

The antidote to this is to do a reality check: unless you have special powers I don't know about, you cannot predict the future. But you can *influence* the future, by acquiring new skills and knowledge that will help you improve.

WHAT NOT TO SAY TO YOURSELF

- "I'll never succeed."
- "This just goes to show I'm doomed to failure."
- "What's the point in trying again? I'm only setting myself up for more disappointment."

WHAT TO SAY INSTEAD

- "Just because I didn't get this opportunity, doesn't mean I can't get the next one."
- "Things will be different next time—because I'll approach them differently."
- "If I learn the lesson and improve, I'll have a better chance next time."

5. COMPARISON

It's natural to compare yourself to others, especially your peer group. When a friend or rival goes on to achieve great things, it would be amazing if you weren't a little envious. So it's easy to fall into the trap of comparing and criticizing yourself for not being as 'good' as they are.

Up to a certain point comparison can be a good thing, inspiring you to emulate others' success. But beyond that point, it becomes a stick to beat yourself with. When that happens, it's better to just focus on yourself. Compare your present performance with your past. Have you improved—even a little bit? How did you do that? Supposing you keep that trend going. How good will you be in a year's time? What do you need to do to keep improving?

WHAT NOT TO SAY TO YOURSELF
- "Look what they've done. I must be useless to be stuck here."
- "If they can do it, why can't I?"

WHAT TO SAY INSTEAD
- "I'm going at my own pace, I'll make it if I keep learning and improving."
- "I'm competing with myself, no one else."
- "I'm going to succeed on my own terms."
- "I'm better than I was this time last year. If I keep stretching myself, I'll be a lot better this time next year."

6. JUST DESERTS

Sometimes we look at other people's success and tell ourselves, "It's just not fair. I don't deserve to be stuck here." When you're in this frame of mind, it seems obvious that you are better than they are, and the world is a very unjust place.

But this is wanting to live in fairyland. As far as we know, there's no such place. You can imagine a world where everybody—especially you—gets exactly what they 'deserve.' But that doesn't mean it's going to come into being anytime soon. Meanwhile, you're stuck in this world, where you still haven't got what you want, however much you think you 'deserve' it.

You can carry on fantasizing about the world of just deserts. Or you can focus on the reality of your situation, and start making plans to show the gatekeepers that you are the best person to be offered the next fabulous opportunity.

WHAT NOT TO SAY TO YOURSELF
- "It's so unfair!"
- "I deserve better than this!"
- "What have they done to deserve success? They must have lied/cheated/bribed/slept with the right person."

WHAT TO SAY INSTEAD
- "I can do better than them, and I'm going to prove it."
- "It feels unfair, but I have to deal with it."
- "Fair play to them, they're obviously doing something right."

7. EXAGGERATION

Rejection can feel like the end of the world. But it isn't. If you're reading this book, the world hasn't ended yet. So try to avoid the natural human tendency to exaggerate, turning a disappointment into a disaster.

When you first get the rejection, feel free to use plenty of exaggeration and expletives! But if you keep on exaggerating and swearing long after the event, you've got a problem. Be honest about your feelings, but don't let your thoughts run away with themselves. Avoid using words like 'worst,' 'absolutely,' 'total,' 'never,' and 'always.' Instead, stick to the facts.

WHAT NOT TO SAY TO YOURSELF
- "This is the absolute worst!"
- "What a total disaster!"
- "I never, ever get what I want!"

- "Why does it *always* happen to me?"

WHAT TO SAY INSTEAD
- "OK I failed again, but it's not the end of the world."
- "This is a big disappointment, but I've bounced back before, so I can do it again."
- "So I'm having a bad run at the moment, but [remind yourself of a previous success]."

Alternatively, keep the exaggeration, but add a humorous twist:
- "The end of the world eh? Who'd have guessed it would be a Tuesday?"
- "Looks like I'm back on Desolation Row. I wonder how long I'll be here this time?"
- "So I'm officially a complete and utter grade A screwup. What else is new?"

CHAPTER 13

Don't think about the black box

Another guaranteed way to make rejection worse is to think about the Black Box.

'Black box' is the scientific term for a system or device that can only be analyzed in terms of its inputs and outputs, because the exact inner workings of its processes are not known.

In electronics, a transistor is a device used to switch or amplify an electric current or signal. The transistor is a form of black box, because you can adjust the inputs to the transistor to get the results you want, without seeing or understanding exactly what happens inside it.

Some financial traders use 'black box programs,' which automatically buy or sell when certain market conditions occur. They don't need to be able to write the programs or understand their inner workings in order to use them.

Behavioral psychologists treat the human mind as a black box. Instead of worrying about what's 'really happening' between the ears, they analyze stimuli (inputs) and behavior (outputs) and try to spot patterns and relationships. I'm not a behavioral psychologist, but this approach can save you a lot of misery when it comes to dealing with rejection.

For example:

Maybe a gatekeeper doesn't even bother to reject you. You never get an answer, even after asking several times. What happened? Were they too busy, too lazy, or even too embarrassed or scared to tell you the bad news?

You'll never know. The answer is inside the Black Box.

Maybe the gatekeeper rejects you but doesn't give you any feedback. So what did you do wrong?

You'll never know. The answer is inside the Black Box.

Maybe they reject you and you get a standard response—a template they just printed out and signed (or got their PA to sign). So how did they decide you belonged in the reject pile?

You'll never know. The answer is inside the Black Box.

Maybe they reject you and give a reason that is factually inaccurate, or an obvious lie. What was the real reason for turning you down?

You'll never know. The answer is inside the Black Box.

Or maybe their behavior is so rude or bizarre that it doesn't make any sense at all, however much you analyze it. What is going on inside their heads? How can they possibly think it's acceptable to behave like this?

You'll never know. The answer is inside the Black Box.

If you want to, you can spend the rest of your life trying to work out what's inside the Black Box.

"I was obviously trying too hard."
"I wasn't trying hard enough."
"I should have asked more questions."
"I didn't ask enough questions."
"I was overqualified."
"I didn't have enough experience."
"They didn't want to hire another man."

"I knew I shouldn't have worn a tie."

"They are idiots!"

"Nepotism."

"They're out to get me."

"I didn't grease the right palms."

You could go on like this forever. But what's the point? Even when you decide on the 'real' reason, deep down you know you're only guessing. The answer is locked inside the Black Box.

As soon as you realize you're dealing with a Black Box, stop trying to analyze its contents.

All you can do is vary your inputs and see if they have any effect on the outputs. If you don't get a response by email, try phoning. If you're not satisfied with the standard rejection letter, write to them and ask for more detailed feedback. If you know someone who knows someone who was involved in the decision, see if they can make a discreet enquiry on your behalf.

And if varying your inputs doesn't make any difference, it's time to move on. Leave the Black Box with its owner, and forget about it. You weren't the right fit this time, for whatever reason, but other opportunities await you, if you persist.

YOUR NEXT STEPS

1. Firstly, train yourself to recognize a Black Box when you see one. Tell-tale signs include: vague, formal, or non-existent communication; stock answers; standard rejection letters; rude or weird behavior.

2. Acknowledge your natural urge to guess what's inside. But remind yourself you'll never know the real answer.

3. Let go of the Black Box. Stop thinking about it. Close your eyes and imagine handing the box back to the gatekeeper, or burying it in the garden, or incinerating it.

4. Use your mindfulness practice to keep yourself focused on the present.

5. Get on with the next stage of your journey.

CHAPTER 14

Are you still in the game?

It's not how many times you get knocked down; it's how many times
you get back up.

Attributed to General George Armstrong Custer. 89

The last stand comes to all of us sooner or later. But before you
get to that point, chances are you'll be knocked down many times.
And there will be a few times when it feels as though you'll never
get back up, never recover, never want to put yourself through
it all again.

But when the dust settles, it's amazing how often you *do* find
the strength to get back up again. Time passes, your wounds
heal, and you get a bit of perspective. And one day—maybe a
few days later, maybe not for months or years—you feel a flicker
of the old enthusiasm come back. You realize with surprise that
you *do* want to put yourself through it all again but make it turn
out differently this time.

For example, you've just been rejected—again—for the kind
of job you've set your heart on. It feels like the end of the world.
You're tempted to give it all up and set your sights lower. But on
looking through the listings the following week, you realize the
world is still turning, vacancies are still arising, and you still have
your resume/portfolio/CV. You're still in the game. And you still
have the desire to win.

Or imagine you're an entrepreneur and your latest product has flopped spectacularly. You invested months in its development—as well as money, time, and stress you couldn't really afford. But nobody bought it. And nobody cared how much you suffered. In the wake of the disaster, you think it's Game Over. But looking at your spreadsheets the following month, you realize you still have enough cash flow to keep the doors open and the lights on. You still have customers who are happy with your other products or services. And you remember an idea you had for a new product... You're still in the game. And you still have the desire to win.

Here's another situation... Say you're a writer and your novel has been rejected by 20 publishers. You've just spent a week in bed with Netflix and industrial quantities of Cheerios/Mars bars/whisky (delete as appropriate). Then one day you look at the curtains and see light around the edges. It must be daytime. You draw the curtains and blink in the sunshine. You realize you still have your manuscript and the list of publishers is not yet exhausted. And there's that book on self-publishing you haven't read yet. Heck, you even have an idea for a new novel that you've been itching to start on... You're still in the game. And you still have the desire to win.

Say you're a performer and you've been rejected for a minor part—not even the one you really wanted—yet again. You're sick of this. You ignore the consoling phone messages from your agent/mother/best friend (delete as appropriate). You neglect your practice routine. You ignore the industry press. Then one day, out of morbid curiosity, you take a peek and see a part advertised. You *know* you could do it. You still have time before the deadline. And you still have your agent's number. You're still in the game. And you still have the desire to win.

No, none of these scenarios is where you *want* to be. You thought it would be quicker and easier than this. You thought you'd have been well on the way to making it by now.

But you are where you are. The world is what it is. And the game is still there to be played—if you still want to.

YOUR NEXT STEPS

1. When you get a big rejection, one that feels like your last stand, don't resist—roll with the punch. Give yourself your allotted 48 hours (or equivalent) to nurse your wounds.

2. When the wound licking time is up, take an inventory of what you need to keep playing the game and chasing the next opportunity: time, money, connections, collaborators etc. Do you still have the necessary?

3. Now ask yourself whether you still have the enthusiasm—is it still there, even if only a tiny flicker?

4. If the enthusiasm is there, ask yourself: "What's the smallest step I could take to rejoin the game?" For example, calling your agent, checking out a job listings site, or opening up your list of publishers.
Make it as small and specific as possible—something you could do in the next 5 minutes. Then go do it.

REJECTION

CHAPTER 15

Is the prize worth the price?

If this were easy, everyone would do it. But everything has a price. If you want to achieve something extraordinary with your life, then rejection is part of the price.

Most people are not willing to pay that price. It hurts too much, or they are too impatient or too proud to put themselves through the 'humiliation' of being turned down again and again.

So… if you can persist in the face of rejection, you are automatically ahead of the pack.

When you stop taking rejection **personally** and accept that it's just part of the process, you start paying the price for success.

But there are no guarantees—otherwise more people would be willing to persist. So you need to keep going in the face of uncertainty as well as rejection, and this puts you in an even smaller category.

But we're not talking about blind persistence. It's only worth paying the price if the ultimate prize is worth it.

In his book *Man's Search for Meaning*, about his experience in a Nazi concentration camp, Viktor Frankl recounts how his vision of the future kept him going: in the midst of the miseries of the camp, he would imagine himself having survived, giving a lecture to an audience about his experience and the lessons he learned from it. The desire to tell that story, to make something positive out of such an awful experience, gave him the strength to carry on—and to tell the story to many, many people, in his lectures and books. Hopefully you'll never have to go through anything as harrowing as Frankl. But you can use this same technique to keep yourself going in your darkest hours.

Next time you are undergoing your latest and most discouraging rejection, pause for a moment and imagine you can see into the future. Picture yourself having come through your trials and achieved your biggest goals, and sharing what you have learned with others.

YOUR NEXT STEPS

1.   Next time you suffer a big rejection and start to wonder if it's worth carrying on, have a look in your crystal ball...

Start by imagining all the good things you will have—a sense of achievement, money, freedom, prestige, opportunities, and so on.

Then imagine the positive difference you will have made to other people through your work.

Next, imagine what it will be like to have the satisfaction of having done it the hard way, overcoming all the obstacles that were put in your path.

Finally, imagine what lessons you will have learned, that you will be glad to share with others.

This is the prize you are pursuing.

2.   Now look at the reality of the situation you are facing. (Be careful not to make it worse than it really is—re-read Chapter 12 to check!)

This is the price you are paying.

3.   Now ask yourself: is the prize worth the price?
If not... give up.
Seriously.

Why put yourself through it for something that's not worth it? Go back to Chapter 4 and rethink your ambitions. Do not pass 'Go' until you have found something worth committing to and putting yourself on the line for.

If the prize *is* worth the price… grit your teeth and get on with it. The sooner you do this and move on, the more chance you have of grasping the glittering prize for real.

NOTE

For inspiration and advice on handling the uncertainty that goes hand in hand with pursuing creative and risky projects, see Jonathan Fields' book *Uncertainty: Turning Fear and Doubt into Fuel for Brilliance* (Portfolio/Penguin, 2011).

CHAPTER 16

You gotta laugh

Humor is a neglected source of resilience. If you can laugh—especially at yourself and your situation—you can persevere.

One of my goals with every coaching and psychotherapy client I have worked with over the years has been to get them to laugh at least once in every session, no matter how horrendous the situation they are dealing with. Firstly, because they need it, and secondly because if they can laugh I know they can change. Laughter helps them break out of their current mindset and see things differently, even if only for a moment. It unlocks their creativity and playfulness. And it makes them feel more human, giving them the strength to persist.

Laughter can help you develop resilience. Next time you're suffering the pain of rejection, imagine sitting down with your best friend over a drink, and telling the story of your latest and most humiliating disaster. Ham it up and exaggerate the worst bits for comic effect. Describe your floundering, incompetent, hilariously bad performance. Do an impression of the gatekeeper as they delivered their withering putdown. And don't forget to include the embarrassing encounter with your rival on the way out, or the dog crap you stepped in on the way home, or any of the other excruciating details that made this whole escapade a tragedy of epic proportions.

When you do this, you let go of your ego, you get out of the 'poor me' way of thinking. You start to see the funny side and get some perspective. This is the beginning of thinking creatively about the situation.

And make sure you call your best friend and tell the tale for real. It's empowering to tell a funny story and make someone laugh. You'll also bond with them and feel less alone. Chances are they'll also start to tell you a funny story about one of their own personal disasters, and you'll realize it's not just you who has to put up with this kind of crap.

Make a habit of doing this, and you will find it helpful even in the midst of the disaster itself. Sitting in the interview room, or holding the rejection letter, or looking in vain for your name on the team sheet, a little part of you will shrug their shoulders and say: "Look on the bright side—this is going to be one hell of a story!"

You've got to laugh. Seriously. It's part of your job. Make it a priority—especially when things don't seem so funny.

YOUR NEXT STEPS

1. Next time you're feeling sorry for yourself, imagine you're sitting with your best friend over your second beer, and tell the 'humorous disaster version' of your situation. Then call your friend and make a date to tell the story for real.

2. In the midst of a disaster, see if you can lighten up—and unlock your creativity—by telling yourself it will be one hell of a story!

3. Spend time with frivolous people who like to have fun. They can teach you plenty—if you're not too proud to learn from them.

4. Make sure you have a stack of comedy DVDs, books, and comics to hand and use them!

CHAPTER 17

Find your tribe

I said the world was mad, and the world said I was mad, and dammit all, they outvoted me.

Attributed to the playwright Nathaniel Lee, on being asked why he was confined to Bedlam insane asylum

Rejection is normal but it doesn't always feel that way. If you're trying to achieve something original, chances are you won't always be surrounded by people who 'get' what you're trying to do. Your friends and family may be well-meaning, but if they don't know what it's like to pursue a dream like yours, they can subtly—or not so subtly—discourage you, by saying things like this:

"Why not get a sensible job and do [insert dream] as a hobby?"

"It's all very well aiming high, but sooner or later you have to live in the real world."

"I guess you need to get it out of your system."

So it's absolutely essential that you find a group of fellow travellers—people who get what you are trying to do, because they are doing something similar.

People who share your enthusiasm and build on your ideas.

People who will introduce you to other people and resources that will help you on your journey.

People who will be there to support you when things are tough, having gone through exactly the same thing themselves.

People who make you feel normal.

For a very long time, I was used to being 'the one who's into poetry.' With the exception of one or two very close friends, virtually no one I knew shared my passion for poetry to anything like the same degree—even among my classmates when I was studying for an English degree! Then one day I walked through the door of the Poetry School in London. To my delight, I found myself in a room full of people who were *just as obsessed as I was*. It felt like coming home.

A few years later, when I got the blogging bug and started connecting and meeting up with other social media users, it felt like we were discovering a whole new world together. These days we take it for granted that we can meet people via Facebook, Twitter, forums, and so on, and meeting up is a natural (if not inevitable) way to extend the relationship. But back then, this was all new and excitingly strange. Each time I went to a bloggers' meetup, for my first meeting with 'friends' I'd known for months online, it felt like we'd been beamed down from the deck of the starship *Enterprise*. This was the future.

But try as I might, it was hard to explain the good news to my friends and colleagues from 'real life.' Their eyes glazed over as I enthused about the brave new world. Then I finished and they would say something like, "But isn't it antisocial to spend all that time on the computer?"

Converting people to your point of view is hard work. Better to accept that some people will never really 'get' your enthusiasms, and to go in search of the people who do. Fortunately I was right about the brave new world—our hyper-connected social networks make it easier than ever to find people who share your passion.

Seth Godin calls these groups 'tribes.' He points out that human beings have organized themselves into tribes for millennia. The old tribes were based on kinship and geography. The new tribes are organized around common passions—music, motorbikes, madrigals, parkour, face painting, fencing, cupcake baking, and so on. When you find your tribe, you plug in to a powerhouse of resilience.

YOUR NEXT STEPS

1.   Who do you already know who shares your passion? Could it help all of you to spend more time together—face-to-face and/or online? Maybe you could organize a regular get-together, or set up a private discussion forum online. Or maybe just make more of an effort to stay in touch via phone and email.

2.   Is there a local group or class dedicated to your passion? As well as checking the usual sources, search on MeetUp.com—an online directory of groups organized by interest and location. When you find a likely group, go along and check it out.

3.   Look for online tribes. Search for forums, Facebook or LinkedIn groups, Google+ circles, and blogs dedicated to your interest. Spend a bit of time lurking to begin with, to check out the vibe and etiquette, then join the conversation.

4.   If you don't find the kind of group you're looking for, why not start one yourself? Advertise the first meeting in your local library, and on sites like CraigsList.org and MeetUp.com. Start a blog or Facebook group and begin reaching out to people.

NOTES

Seth Godin, *Tribes: We need you to lead us* (Piatkus, 2008)
The Poetry School: www.poetryschool.com

CHAPTER 18

How to fix it next time

Insanity: doing the same thing over and over again and expecting different results.

Albert Einstein   103

There's no point getting back up if you leave yourself open to the same left hook every time. You'll keep getting floored until you can't take any more. Once you're back on your feet after being hit by rejection, ask yourself what you can learn from the experience.

Here are some of the most common reasons for rejection, and how to fix them next time round.

1. YOU DIDN'T MEET THE MINIMUM CRITERIA

This should go without saying, but—having been on the other side of the fence, as a gatekeeper myself a few times—I can assure you it doesn't.

When I was editing the magazine *Magma Poetry*, our website clearly stated that email submissions should be pasted in the body of the email, with a maximum of six poems per poet. So no prizes for guessing what kind of impression it made when someone sent in a Word document with over 50 pages of poems.

On my blog at lateralaction.com, I've posted a set of guidelines for guest writers and yet I still get submissions via the form on the same page, that ignore the guidelines.

When you apply for an opportunity, you need to check the application guidelines:

- Do they take speculative applications?
- Do they take email submissions?
- How many copies do you need to send?
- What's the closing date?
- What file formats are acceptable?
- How many images do they want in a portfolio?
- Is there an age limit?

I know this sounds blindingly obvious, but—as any gatekeeper will tell you—there are plenty of people who don't do it. Guidelines are there for a reason—to make the process easier for the gatekeeper. Create an unnecessary problem for them, and you make it harder for them to accept you.

HOW TO FIX IT NEXT TIME
Follow the instructions to the letter!

2. YOU DIDN'T GIVE THEM WHAT THEY WERE REALLY LOOKING FOR

Every gatekeeper makes his or her decision based on certain key criteria—if you can figure out what these are, the task of convincing them becomes a lot easier.

Did you get any real feedback with your rejection? By 'real feedback' I don't mean standard stuff like, "We receive a high volume of high-quality applications..." I mean feedback about specific things you did or didn't do, and why that was important in their eyes.

If you can get this it's gold dust, because it tells you the rules of the game they are playing. Once you know the rules, you can decide whether it's a game you want to play and how to win. Or you may decide you want to play a different game, and look elsewhere in future.

HOW TO FIX IT NEXT TIME

Make it your business to find out what the key criteria are before you apply and to make it obvious to the gatekeepers that you fulfill them.

Sometimes the gatekeepers spell out their criteria in the application instructions. As well as the minimum requirement, they tell you exactly what they are looking for. And I'm not talking about qualifications! Most gatekeepers are looking for something that is *less obvious* than letters after your name, such as proven experience in a specific role; the ability to solve particular kinds of problems; the achievement of measurable, memorable results; or the ability to collaborate as well as execute.

The next step is to research the gatekeepers. Read their books, articles, interviews, blog posts, even tweets and Facebook update. Do you know anyone who knows them or has worked with them? If so, ask about them. Keep asking yourself what all this tells you about their taste, their values, their influences, their passions, and their pet hates. And what does it tell you about their likely criteria for judging your application?

When I applied to Oxford to do an English degree, the college prospectus described the academic specialisms of the two dons who were to interview me. One of them was an authority on Anglo-Saxon literature, a part of the syllabus many students dreaded. But having been captivated by the story of Beowulf in translations and retellings, I was actually *looking forward* to reading the original text—so I made a point of saying so in the interview. I wasn't faking it—I was (and still am) genuinely enthusiastic about Anglo-Saxon poetry. I doubt it was the critical factor in their decision to give me a place, but I'm sure it didn't do me any harm. And if I hadn't done my research, I might not have thought to mention it.

Don't wait until the end for feedback—if you have contact with the gatekeepers during the process, they may well be giving you feedback all the way through, whether they intend to or not. When you're talking to them, notice when they sit up and pay attention, versus looking bored or indifferent. Notice what they ask about and what they don't ask about.

Shortly after leaving college, I was being interviewed for some freelance proofreading work. I noticed the editor's eyes glaze over as I waffled on about my love of literature and writing. Clearly I was doing a great job of screwing up the interview. Then I happened to mention that spelling or punctuation mistakes jumped out at me when I was reading a book, and I found them really irritating. Suddenly she sat up and beamed: "That's *exactly* what I want to hear!" Even I could take the hint at that point, and I reeled off a few more of my pet hates when it came to sloppy writing and editing—and got the job.

3. YOU WERE CHASING THE WRONG OPPORTUNITY

Years ago I had a meeting with the owner of a prestigious West End sports club, with a view to offering hypnotherapy services to his clientele. I'd done some really good work with a few professional golfers and tennis players, so I was confident I could do a good job here. The owner asked me to give him a session so he could see how I worked, and it went... OK. Not an obvious disaster, but

nothing to get excited over either. So I wasn't ~~s~~
polite 'thanks but no thanks' letter a few days]

At the time it was disappointing, but on ref
wouldn't have been happy or successful in that
was a nice guy, the facilities were superb, and the ~~...~~
was very professional. Looking back, I realized my gut instinct
had been telling me the club didn't feel like home to me. I would
never have fitted in there.

That taught me to focus my efforts working with people with
whom I had a natural affinity—the artists, creatives, and entrepreneurs who were my most enthusiastic clients, and the most
fun to work with.

My first sales call under my new identity was to Chris Arnold,
a partner in an ad agency and an ex-creative director at Saatchi
and Saatchi. The first thing he asked when I picked up the phone
was: "Do you do anything creative yourself, or are you one of
those consultants who just tell other people how to be creative?"

When I told him I wrote poetry he burst out laughing and
said, "I've never had a sales call from a poet before! Why don't
you come in for coffee?"

A few days later, Chris welcomed me to his office. Music was
playing, the walls were covered in pictures, people were wearing
T-shirts and jeans. There was an electric guitar in the corner of
the room. I instantly felt at home. That meeting led to several
speaking gigs at conferences Chris organized, and we are still
friends to this day.

HOW TO FIX IT NEXT TIME

If you receive positive feedback on your performance, but get
rejected in spite of it, maybe you're just applying for the wrong
kind of opportunity. Or maybe you get a feeling that your face
doesn't fit. You could struggle to break in and be accepted. Or

could go in search of your own crowd—people who will smile with recognition when they see what you're all about, and welcome you with open arms.

4. YOU'RE NOT GOOD ENOUGH (YET)

Let's be honest. Sometimes we just aren't there yet, in terms of our ability. The bar is raised a lot higher than we can reach—for now.

In my early teens I used to fence with a foil. I enjoyed lessons at the local club, so when the instructor asked if I'd like to enter a competition, I thought "Why not?" Within sixty seconds of stepping onto the piste under the eye of the judges I was taught a short, sharp lesson in the art of swordsmanship. Even as my defense was brushed aside and I felt my rib cage jabbed again and again by my opponent's foil, I remember admiring the sheer speed and precision of his movements. There was a lot more to this than I had realized!

I had a similar experience—if not quite so brutal—when I first discovered the Poetry School in London. I'd previously attended a few writing groups, and without blowing my own trumpet, I'd usually found myself near the top of the class in terms of ability and experience. But on this day, I realized the standard was a lot higher than I'd encountered before, and I was definitely in the bottom half. It was a bit of a shock, but once I got over that I felt a surge of enthusiasm. I realized that the teacher, Mimi Khalvati, was encouraging me to aim a lot higher than I had done before and it was an exciting prospect.

HOW TO FIX IT NEXT TIME

If it turns out you're not as good as the competition, you have two options: give up or get better. There's no shame in giving up if that's what you really want to do. Only resolve to get better if you're really excited about the idea of putting in the work required.

5. YOU DIDN'T DO YOURSELF JUSTICE

I've left this one till last, not because it's the least important, but because so many people go wrong by failing to take enough account of what the gatekeepers are looking for. But sometimes you can be so worried about pleasing other people that you lose touch with your own instincts, and don't express your talent to the full. The work you did may have been OK, but it wasn't the real you.

HOW TO FIX IT NEXT TIME

Ask yourself whether you are happy with the way you performed. If not, what was missing? What do you need to do next time, to stay true to yourself?

If you're struggling, ask someone who knows you well for their opinion. Even if they weren't there to see you perform, they can probably pick up quite a bit from your words and expressions as you tell them about it. And they may well have some valuable advice to give you.

YOUR NEXT STEPS

Next time you're rejected, run through these questions, to review what went wrong and what you could do differently next time.

1. Did you meet the minimum requirements? If not, be meticulous next time!

2.   Did you fail to identify the real criteria? If so, do more research next time.

Did you fail to demonstrate that you met these criteria? If so, make sure you signpost them to the next gatekeeper.

3.   Were you chasing the wrong opportunity? Did you feel at home with the kind of people you encountered? Should you apply somewhere very different next time?

4.   Were you just not good enough? If so, do you want to give up or get better?

If the latter, either study and practice on your own or find a teacher who will help you improve.

5.   Did you fail to do yourself justice? If so, how will you stay true to yourself next time?

NOTES

Chris Arnold now runs Creative Orchestra (and has three guitars and two pianos in the office). www.creativeorchestra.com

Mimi Khalvati: www.mimikhalvati.co.uk

The Poetry School: www.poetryschool.com

CHAPTER 19

Play the numbers game

Imagine you're an actor who has been out of work for months. The landlord's patience is at breaking point, not to mention your long-suffering partner. And today you have an audition for a part that could solve all your problems. You know you can play the part and you're desperate to do yourself justice. But this is the only audition you have, and everything is riding on it. It feels like your last chance.

How confident are you of delivering your very best performance?

Now imagine you're just as short of cash, but today's audition is just one of half a dozen you have lined up, any one of which could put you back in the black and back in everyone's good books. On the way to the audition, you get a call from your agent urging you not to agree to anything even if it goes brilliantly—she's just found another opportunity she thinks could be perfect for you.

Now how confident are you of doing yourself justice?

Maybe you thrive on pressure and like to live on the edge. But typically, the more options you have, the more relaxed you are about any one of them. Which paradoxically means you will perform better, and have a higher chance of success in each instance. So even if you only want to boost your confidence, it makes sense to play the numbers game, by making sure your 'opportunity funnel' is constantly filled with new options.

Sadly, not everyone is going to love your work, even if it is amazing. You sometimes have to knock on lots of doors before you'll find someone willing to give you a chance. But the more you put it out there, the more chances you have of finding the people who *do* love it.

Start with a list—of the gatekeepers, companies, publications, agencies, or other hubs around which opportunities cluster. Then work through it, first researching how to approach them, then gritting your teeth and making the approaches. Assume you will have to hear a lot of 'no's before you hear your first 'yes.' That will help you prepare for the worst, and make the surprise all the sweeter if you get an early win.

The numbers game is another reason for finding and hanging out with your tribe—the more people you know on the scene, the more likely it is that *your* name will crop up in conversation next time a new opportunity is discussed.

YOUR NEXT STEPS

1. Make a list of all the potential opportunities you have right now. Next to each one, write the next step you are going to take towards making it happen, including the date.

Use whatever system is easiest for you—a notebook, a Word document, a spreadsheet, or contact management software. Personally I'm a fan of Bento, as it allows me to organize data with the flexibility of a spreadsheet, but to display it in nice-looking templates instead of the hideousness of Excel. See the Resources page for this book for some other options: lateralaction.com/ resilience-resources

2. Now make a list of all the different people and places you can apply to for more opportunities—publishers, sports clubs, agen-

cies, companies, trials, competitions etc. Research the application process for each one.

3.   Set up a system for applying for opportunities. Do it however you like, as long as it includes the following elements:

- Regular times for searching for new opportunities.
- A methodical approach to preparing each application.
- Tracking the progress of every application.
- If you can only make one application at a time—e.g. sending out a manuscript to publishers who don't allow simultaneous submissions—make sure you have the next application all lined up and ready to be sent out the moment you receive the next rejection.

Your aim is to keep your system in perpetual motion—constantly identifying and applying for new opportunities.

4.   Make a list of the most important gatekeepers and influencers in your field—the kind of people who could send opportunities your way, if they knew and cared who you were. Research each of them thoroughly.

Pick one or two whose ideas resonate for you, and look for opportunities to connect with them via your network—online and offline. Read their blogs and leave comments. Go to their lectures and ask questions. Read their books and write about their ideas online. Follow them on social networks, where etiquette allows—following them on Twitter is probably a good idea, asking to be Facebook friends, not so much. LinkedIn is particularly good at helping you check whether any of your contacts know them.

Look out for opportunities they advertise. If they are open to speculative applications, then approach them yourself—with a meticulously prepared pitch.

5.   Make time to hang out with the tribe you identified in Chapter 17. DON'T keep hustling your peers for opportunities—that's a big turn off. Remember, *the purpose of networking is to build your network*, not to close a deal in every conversation. Focus on making a genuine connection with people and look for opportunities to help *them*, and eventually the opportunities will trickle through to you as well—even if it takes a while.

CHAPTER 20

Narrow the odds

I once built a business by cold calling. I took a deep breath and dialed my way through a list of HR directors' phone numbers, asking them whether they had a need for my company's training courses.

During that time I listened to a lot of tapes of extroverted American sales gurus—guys like Zig Ziglar and Brian Tracy, who were the complete opposite of my diffident English poetic self. It was a way of deliberately stretching my personality in a new direction. I was never going to be as hyper as Power Sales Guy, but it helped me get into a more extroverted state before I made the calls. One of the sales mantras I heard from the gurus was, "You have to hear a lot of 'no's before you hear the word 'yes'!" When you adopt this mindset, you *welcome* rejections, because each one takes you closer to the next acceptance.

It worked. After several months of dogged persistence, I found a few needles in the haystack, landing some big contracts that transformed our business. And I can assure you cold calling is a great way to develop a thick skin for rejection! I wouldn't say I ever got to the point of enjoying it, but after making several hundred calls, the 'no's felt more routine than personal, and the 'yes's that led to meetings and new business made it all worthwhile.

Looking back, relying on cold calling was a stupid way to build a business. I'm embarrassed to admit that at the time I didn't know the difference between marketing (earning the attention and trust of potential customers) and sales (closing the deal). I thought they were just different names for the same thing, so I steeled myself and dialed my way through the list. But in spite of being stupid, it worked. A bit like amateur surgery—thankfully nobody died, but it was pretty uncomfortable and left bigger scars than was strictly necessary.

Playing the numbers game is all very well, but you can save yourself a lot of time and effort if you begin by asking yourself how you can narrow the odds. Which is what I did with my next business...

First I narrowed the field by deciding to specialize in the creative industries—since I was passionate about creativity, and my best work had been done with artists and other creative professionals.

Then I went to college and did a Masters Degree in Creative and Media Enterprises. By the time I'd finished, I knew a hell of a lot more about marketing. And there weren't many aspects of creativity and creative business I hadn't researched and thought hard about. So when I was in front of the right people, I had a much better understanding of their business and the industry they were operating in—which meant I had a much better chance of closing the deal.

I made an effort to get out to networking events, drinking vast quantities of coffee and meeting new people. The more people who knew about me, the better the chances of my name coming up in conversations about the kind of problems I could solve.

I also focused my efforts online, as I figured I could connect with more people more efficiently than trying to meet them all one at a time. I started blogging with the idea of attracting coaching and training clients in London. Then I realized most of my readers were scattered across the globe, and I could greatly expand my options if I found a way to sell things to people in other countries.

I started coaching clients via webcam, which meant all I needed to do was co-ordinate time zones in order to work with clients on the other side of the world. I also developed and sold e-learning courses. I discovered there were even companies who were prepared to fly me across the world to deliver training workshops. With the whole planet to choose from, I now have much better odds of getting on the radar of potential clients.

These days, my sales cycle is a lot more efficient than when I started:

- I focus on a very particular kind of client.
- Because I know a lot more about solving their very specific problems, I convert a lot more leads into sales.
- Casting my net worldwide makes it easier to find enough of them.

I'm still playing the numbers game. I reach thousands of people every week via my blogs, mailing list, and social networks. But I've done a lot to narrow the odds—which means I find more opportunities with less effort.

You can do the same: decide who you *really* want to connect with, and make a concerted effort to get on their radar, while at the same time acquiring the skills and knowledge that will make you extremely valuable to them. Don't try to be all things to all people. Decide what you want to do and make yourself so good at it that you are the obvious choice for the people who matter.

When I started out, I was competing with hundreds of business coaches, and when I took a good look in the mirror, I realized there wasn't anything obvious that made me stand out from them. But I don't know many business coaches who specialize in creativity and online marketing, and who also write poetry. For the people who find that an attractive combination, I'm the obvious choice.

And make the world your oyster. You may think the online world isn't suited to your particular talents or industry (I know I did). But set your skepticism aside and start exploring.

YOUR NEXT STEPS

1.   Decide what you are going to specialize in. Take time to think about it from different angles. Just because *you* enjoy doing something, will anyone pay you to do it? On the other hand, just because there are plenty of opportunities in a particular field, are you passionate enough about it to do your best work there?

Ask yourself:

- What are you most passionate about?
- What are you best at?
- Who do you most like working with?
- What are people most eager to pay you for?

2.   Make yourself an expert. Tell yourself there's no reason why you shouldn't become the best in the world at your particular specialism. It's humanly possible and you are a human.

Depending on your field, there may be courses, qualifications, apprenticeships, or internships that will teach you what you need to know. You may find a private tutor, coach, or mentor who can help. Or it may be something you can only learn by practice. Whatever it takes, resolve to find the time, money, energy, and dedication to do it.

3.   Focus on the right people. This could be as clear-cut as a particular industry or market niche. Or it could be people who share your interests, passions, attitudes, or values. Remember the tips on finding your tribe in Chapter 17 and getting on the radar of gatekeepers in Chapter 19.

4.   Get online. Even if you live in a big city, there will only be a few million people in your immediate vicinity. That might feel like a lot, but there are 7 billion people on this planet—over 2 billion of them are already connected to the internet (lateralaction.com/internet-users), a number that has doubled in the last five years and is still rising fast. Drawing on a much bigger pool of potential connections will exponentially increase your chances of success. (Plus if you don't do it, you're at a disadvantage compared to the people who do...)

Social networks, such as Twitter, Facebook, LinkedIn, Google+, are a good place to start (see my guide 'The Top 10 Social Networks for Creative People': lateralaction.com/articles/social-networks-for-creatives). But anyone can fill out a profile in less than an hour, which makes it hard to stand out. Think about what you can create and publish—as a blog, newsletter, podcast, video, or images—that will set you apart and establish you as an expert in your field.

NOTE

"Number of Internet users worldwide reaches two billion: UN," *The Independent*, 26 January 2011, lateralaction.com/internet-users

REJECTION

CHAPTER 21

The day I tipped the scales in my favor

It's a truism that success takes a long time. But I can also remember the day my fortunes changed.

I was at home in my flat, having just put the phone down. I'd been cold calling for months, working my way through the list of phone numbers, trying to reach decision-makers. I'd had plenty of meetings, but no new business to show for it.

But the call I'd just finished wasn't a cold call. The previous month, I'd traveled half the length of England for a meeting with the HR director of a large company. She requested a proposal for a pilot seminar, with the aim of rolling out an extensive program. I'd spent several days writing the proposal.

But when I rang to discuss it on the date arranged, she was unavailable. I rang several more times. Finally the phone was picked up by a PA, who reluctantly put me through to one of the director's colleagues. She seemed outraged that I expected a response. "*We'll be in touch if we need anything else from you,*" she snapped, and hung up. I felt humiliated.

At that moment, I realized I could have any excuse I wanted for giving up.

No one would blame me. My business partners knew how tough it was. Ditto my family and friends. I was pretty well guaranteed sympathy if I admitted failure. But I didn't want excuses, sympathy, or failure. I wanted success. So I promised myself *I would do whatever it took to make this business work*.

I stopped asking myself whether I was wasting my time, and whether it was possible. Instead, I started asking myself *how* I could make it happen. I read everything I could about the corporate sales process. I developed a thicker skin for rejection. And one day, I walked out of a meeting into the sunshine and rang my business partners to tell them I had closed a deal.

In this case, the pilot actually happened. And it actually led to an extended program that brought in more money than all my previous clients put together.

A few months into the program, I asked my client what had made him choose us. "Well, it took several months for us to decide," he said, "and you were the only guy who kept calling me all the way through. So it seemed only fair to give you a chance." In other words, what had separated me from the competition was *persistence*.

So in spite of being clueless about marketing and sales when I set out, I succeeded through sheer persistence and a willingness to learn along the way. And that persistence came from the decision I made at my lowest ebb, when instead of giving up, I chose to commit.

At that moment, I tipped the scales in my favor.

You've probably realized by now that there's no magic bullet, no magic formula, no foolproof system that leads to success. And no infallible guru to tell you what to do. The real magic happens inside, in your mind and heart. Only you can commit to making your dream happen, whatever obstacles stand in your way. Only you can turn that key.

CHAPTER 22

Make rejection irrelevant

The opposite of rejection isn't acceptance—it's *attraction*.

The world is changing. In the past this is how opportunities were allocated:

1. A gatekeeper advertised the opportunity.
2. Applicants applied.
3. The gatekeeper accepted or rejected them.

Now you can reverse this process:

1. You advertise yourself.
2. Gatekeepers approach you with opportunities.
3. Both of you decide whether you want to work together.

In this world, rejection becomes irrelevant. Since you're not applying, no-one can reject you. And the other party isn't applying either, just approaching you to see if there's a good fit between your skills, priorities, and resources, and theirs. It's a more equal conversation between potential partners—and if there's not a good fit, it's no big deal. At the very least, you both have a potentially valuable new connection in your network.

This is the world I entered by blogging. Realizing cold calling was a monkey-with-a-typewriter way to build a business, I decided to advertise myself by blogging tips and inspiration for creative people. It took a while to figure out an approach that worked, but a few months in, I had a steadily growing audience of subscribers—and the enquiries started to come in. Creative directors—people who would never have taken my phone calls a few months earlier—started emailing and calling *me*, inviting me in to talk about how I could help them. When I arrived, I didn't have to make the usual sales pitch—they asked me what I would *advise*.

A few years down the line, it's a lot more fun to check my email inbox than it used to be.

Some of the emails are coaching enquiries, from people across the globe. Some of them are notifications of sales of my ebooks and e-learning courses. Others are consulting enquiries from organizations, mostly in the UK but also from abroad: in the last twelve months I've worked on-site for clients on three different continents, including speaking at one of the biggest design conferences in the United States, HOW Design in Boston. Over and above the business benefits, every day I hear from interesting, inspiring, charming, and funny people spread across the four corners of the globe.

As well as new clients and customers, I receive unexpected offers and opportunities. I've been offered several book deals. (I decided to publish this one myself, but it's always nice to be asked.) I spent two years running a business in partnership with Brian Clark and Tony Clark, two partners in Copyblogger Media (www. copyblogger.com), a successful online marketing business. Brian and Tony are in the States and I am here in the UK. We've never met in person, but I'm sure we'll get round to it at some point.

None of this would have happened if I hadn't decided to take the initiative and build myself an **opportunity magnet**—which in my case was a blog.

If you are truly sick of rejection and want to make it irrelevant in your life, then I suggest you start building your own opportunity magnet.

An opportunity magnet has several characteristics:

- It's a self-started project. No one will give you the incentive of a reward or a deadline.
- It takes time.
- It will feel like a waste of time some days, and demand plenty of resilience.
- It will become more valuable as time goes on—bringing you more and better opportunities with less effort.
- It will take on a life of its own, because of the contributions made by other people.
- It will connect you up with a vast network of people and possibilities.
- It will connect you with your sense of purpose.
- It will be one of the most rewarding things you ever do.

So what shape will your opportunity magnet take? A blog is an obvious format—it's served me well and I would encourage you to consider it. It helps if you're good at writing, but you don't need to be Shakespeare—you can go a long way with enthusiasm, something valuable to share, and a willingness to learn. If you're a better speaker than writer, maybe podcasting or videos would work better for you.

But it doesn't need to be an online project. Maybe you'd rather put on a live event, or a series of meetings or classes. Maybe you want to write a book, or record a film or album, or make a piece of software as your calling card. And opportunity magnets are not just for the self-employed. You could build one to help your career, by establishing yourself as a thought leader in your industry.

A great example of an event-based opportunity magnet is Speaking Out, started by Laura North in London:

Speaking Out helps people, particularly women, get more comfortable and confident with public speaking. I started it because

I was terrified of public speaking and avoided it for many years. But I realized that I was missing out on opportunities and saw that there were a lot of other people in the same boat. I also noticed that there were far more men than women speaking at the conferences that I was going to.

Running Speaking Out has illustrated my theory that if you speak in public then you attract opportunities. A woman who worked for the Mayor's Office was in the audience at my first event. She really enjoyed it and invited me to put on my second event at City Hall. On another occasion, I did a presentation about Speaking Out and was offered funding to develop a new project, even though I wasn't pitching for any funding.

I keep getting requests to do public speaking—ironic as it's the one thing I was avoiding for so long!

Laura North, Speaking Out, SpeakingOutEvents.com

Whatever format you choose for your opportunity magnet, make sure it has these three essential qualities:

1. **SUSTAINABILITY**—you are passionate about it, and can see yourself doing it for a long time.
2. **VISIBILITY**—it will get you on the radar of the right people.
3. **SIGNIFICANCE**—it will make a positive difference to your field, over and above the opportunities that come to you personally.

When you start building your opportunity magnet, you stop waiting to be invited, accepted or rejected, and take the initiative. You throw your hat in the ring, announce your presence to the world, and ask it to pay attention. You lift your head above the parapet. And when you do that, of course, you expose yourself to criticism...

YOUR NEXT STEPS

1.   ARE YOU UP FOR THE CHALLENGE?
Consider the facts that there are no guarantees, you will have to invest a lot of time and effort up front, and you will probably have to go up a few blind alleys before you find a way to make it work.

Do you still want to build an opportunity magnet?

2.   TAKE THE LEAD
This is the most important step. When you start building something of your own instead of applying to others, you stop being an applicant and start becoming a leader. Like all the best things in life, it's both exciting and scary.

Becoming a leader is partly an attitude of mind—instead of waiting for others, start thinking what needs to be done. It's also a habit of action—once you have an idea you are passionate about, start planning and doing to make it happen.

3.   BRING SOMETHING NEW TO THE TABLE
Ask yourself:

- Who do I want to reach?
- What difference do I want to make to them?
- What's in it for them to join me on the journey?

Once you've identified the 'tribe' of people you want to help, do some research about the kind of publications they subscribe to (magazines, newsletters, blogs etc.) and the kind of events they attend (gigs, exhibitions, conferences etc.).

As well as noting what is already popular with this group of people, ask yourself what's *missing*: is there an obvious gap in the market that you could fill by offering something new?

4. PICK A PLATFORM THAT SUITS YOU—AND YOUR AUDIENCE

I'm a writer. I also have a young family and want to spend as much time as possible with them. So blogging is a natural fit for me. My audience love to read, it's a great way to rise up the search engine rankings, and it allows me to reach a worldwide audience of tens of thousands a week from my home office.

But maybe you're a better speaker, musician, or artist than a writer. Maybe you think there's no substitute for meeting face-to-face. Maybe you want to reach people who prefer watching video to reading, or who do their networking in person, not online.

In choosing the format of your opportunity magnet, look for the best fit between your talents (writing, speaking, singing, coding, etc.) and what your prospective audience likes to do (watch video, read, socialize, play games etc.).

Here are some of the options:

- blog
- newsletter
- podcast
- videocast
- webinar
- online forum
- live networking event
- conference
- live workshop
- book
- recorded music
- film
- software app

5. GIVE MORE THAN YOU ASK FOR

Generosity is key to making your opportunity magnet work. Make it freely available, or at least have a low-cost version of it. And give away something of real value—your knowledge, skills, ideas, contacts. As Brian Clark of Copyblogger.com likes to say, if you feel like you're giving away too much for free, you've probably got it about right!

At my website lateralaction.com I not only publish a free blog, I give away a free 26-week careers course for creative people. Of the thousands of people who sign up, most will never buy anything from me, but enough of them do to keep my business growing. You could say it's an inefficient way to grow a business, but I've always made my living by helping people, and I love the fact that the technology allows me to achieve my goals by helping thousands of people to reach theirs.

An opportunity magnet has a two-way current—you create opportunities for yourself by doing it for other people first. When you do it right, it takes on a life of its own. It starts pulsing and creating unexpected connections. Opportunities come to you, as surely as iron filings line up in the force field of a magnet.

So when in doubt, err on the side of giving too much—when it comes to an opportunity magnet, it's less risky than giving too little.

6. CONNECT PEOPLE

Opportunity magnets attract something more valuable than iron filings: people. So make it part of your mission to facilitate connections and conversations and relationships between members of your audience, not just with yourself and them.

If you're organizing a live event, this will happen naturally. If you're working online, there are several public venues where you can host and contribute to conversations, such as blog comments, forums, and social networks. And make it your business to connect people behind the scenes as well, by looking out for people who could benefit from knowing each other and making introductions via email.

7. GET PERMISSION TO STAY IN TOUCH

There's no point attracting people if they just go away again. You need a way to stay in touch. Which means you need to earn people's trust and gain their permission to contact them.

Marketer Seth Godin describes permission marketing as: "the privilege (not the right) of delivering anticipated, personal, and relevant messages to people who actually want to get them." (sethgodin.typepad.com/seths_blog/2008/01/permission-mark. html) In other words, you should be sending them messages that are so valuable (to them) and so relevant (to them) that they will be happy to hear from you—and they'll miss you if you stop contacting them.

When it comes to getting people to pay attention to your messages, it's hard to beat email. Most people check their email every day, even at weekends. They will at least scan the subject line of every email that lands in their inbox. The same cannot be said of every tweet or Facebook post from their 'friends.' So if you really want people to come to your event, or read your blog post, or take any kind of action, it pays to get permission to contact them via email.

Because email is so powerful, it is easily and widely abused. Here are some essential tips for building a mailing list that adds value for *everyone* who comes into contact with it:

- **Never add someone's email address to the list yourself!** Apart from being rude, this is illegal in many places. Always ask for permission first.
- **Include a one-click 'unsubscribe' link in every email you send.**
- **Use a professional email service** that will automate the signup and delivery process and help you manage the list. See the *Resilience* resources page for recommended services: lateralaction.com/resilience-resources

- **Invite people to sign up to the list** and explain what's in it for them—on your website, when you speak in public, when you meet them in person.
- **Remember: give more than you ask for!** Send them valuable information, tips and advice; share the news that matters to *them*; surprise them by delivering more than you promised.
- **Don't just treat it like a sales channel!** (Or a 'request channel' if you're not selling anything.) Sales messages and requests are fine, as long as they are super-relevant and they aren't all you send. Otherwise people will unsubscribe in droves.
- **Write compelling subject lines.** Most people scan their inbox, so a message like 'April newsletter' is hardly going to inspire them to open your email. Give them a reason to open it, with a subject line that explains (a) what's inside and (b) why it matters to them. For example, 'Tango for beginners—free class Monday 12th April,' or 'Four simple strategies for tackling any problem.' To learn how to write better subject lines, read Brian Clark's series on Writing Magnetic Headlines: www.copyblogger.com/magnetic-headlines

8. MAKE IT SUSTAINABLE

Building an opportunity magnet takes time, and the rewards are not immediate, so you need three things to sustain your efforts long enough to see them bear fruit:

- **PASSION**—You MUST be passionate about the subject and about connecting with your audience, in order to put in the time and effort required to make it a success.
- **ORGANISATION**—Finding time for a medium-to-long-term project is rarely easy. To do it, you'll need to be good at organizing your time—my free ebook *Time Management for Creative People* will help you: www.wishfulthinking.co.uk/time-management-ebook

- **SUPPORT**—As your project grows, it may well get to the stage where it's impossible for you to run it all by yourself. Fortunately, this can only happen if you're attracting plenty of enthusiastic people who share your passion—so don't be too proud to ask for help!

9. BRACE YOURSELF...

You will be doing something wrong if you don't get plenty of praise and enthusiasm from the people you have set out to help. Enjoy it. And brace yourself for the inevitable criticism—we'll look at how to handle that in the next section...

NOTES

Speaking Out: SpeakingOutEvents.com

Seth Godin, *Permission Marketing: Turning Strangers into Friends and Friends into Customers*, (Pocket Books, new edition 2007)

CRITICISM

CHAPTER 23

Dare to be a tall poppy

The seventh and last King of Rome was Lucius Tarquinius Superbus, known as Tarquin the Proud. According to the historian Livy, one day the King received a messenger from his son Sextus Tarquinius, asking for advice on how to deal with the city of Gabii, east of Rome.

Tarquin said nothing to the messenger, but went out into the garden and swept his stick in an arc, cutting off the heads of the tallest poppies growing there.

Puzzled, the messenger returned to his master and reported what he had seen. On hearing the story, Sextus grasped his father's meaning and ordered the deaths of all the most powerful men in Gabii.

The memory of that bloody episode survives today as **tall poppy syndrome**—the idea that people who distinguish themselves from the crowd by their talents or achievements are liable to be resented and criticized (or worse).

As soon as you try to achieve something original, you start to stick out like a tall poppy. Rise too high and some people will inevitably start itching to cut you down to size. But it's the nature of some poppies to grow tall, just as it's your nature to dream big.

Dare to be a tall poppy.

NOTE

Titus Livius, *History of Rome*, Book 1, lateralaction.com/livy

CHAPTER 24

Is constructive criticism a myth?

"Can I give you some constructive criticism?"

Seven of the most terrifying words you will ever hear. This is partly because we all have our own definition of 'constructive' and partly because, however well-intentioned the critique, very few people are good at delivering it. And partly because some people use it as a convenient term to take you down a peg or two while pretending to be nice.

For one reason or another, criticism usually feels a lot more 'constructive' to the giver than the receiver.

So is 'constructive criticism' a contradiction in terms?

I'll put my cards on the table and say I believe criticism *can be* constructive—in fact, it's essential if you want to become outstanding. But because it can mean so many different things, I'll start this section by clarifying what I mean by different types of criticism:

- Feedback
- Constructive criticism
- Destructive criticism
- Personal abuse

FEEDBACK

This is a nice neutral sounding term. Business coach Steve Roesler points out that it got into circulation via the aerospace industry:

> Feedback started as a term used to describe the signals sent from a rocket back to Earth in order to determine the accuracy of the rocket's course. By tracking speed and trajectory, ground crews could determine when and where to make corrections.
>
> At some point in time, the term Feedback was incorporated into business language as a way to talk about performance. And, as in rocket flight, it has been determined that the best way for a person to stay "on course" is to assess where one stands at any given moment in relation to the task or goal at hand.
>
> Here's the really important point: The chances of impacting performance increase with frequency and timeliness of feedback. That implies the need for ongoing "How are we doing?" conversations. It's our best chance at knowing whether we're on track or not.
>
> *Steve Roesler, "What, Why and How: Feedback" www.allthings-worksplace.com/2012/05/what-why-and-how-feedback.html*

Unfortunately, the term feedback has taken on a lot of negative connotations, effectively becoming a code word for criticism. As Steve says, its meaning has morphed from "Here's how I think we're doing" to "Here's what you need to correct." Which is why, when clients ask people like Steve and me for tips on 'giving feedback,' they generally aren't talking about praise.

But for my purposes here, I want to reclaim the neutral meaning of feedback, so that it refers to **any process that raises your awareness of your performance and helps you improve it.**

It can take various forms:

- A genuinely neutral, observational description of your performance, e.g. "the ball landed two inches inside the back line."
- A video or audio recording of your performance.
- An instruction that directs your attention to a specific aspect of your performance.
- For example, "As you speak, I want you to notice the sensation in your throat, whether it feels relaxed or tense."
- A question that directs attention to a specific aspect of your performance. For example, "How do you feel you handled the dialogue in that chapter?"
- A measurement of some specific aspect of your performance. For example, the average minutes per mile in your last run, or the percentage of visitors to your sales page who made a purchase.

Feedback is often sadly neglected in favor of advice.

To observers it seems *so obvious* what the performer should do differently that we can't help telling them. But being told what to do isn't always the best way to learn. For one thing, most of us have a natural resistance to it (I know I do). And for another, it's far more powerful to see—really *see*—something for yourself than to be told about it by someone else.

This is why many experienced coaches and teachers see their job as creating the conditions for the performer to see and feel for themselves where they are going wrong. When I first started giving presentations, I would occasionally receive feedback that I wasn't very expressive, and could do with showing more emotion. But it wasn't until someone showed me a video of myself presenting that I saw it for myself and laughed. After that, it became obvious what I needed to change and much easier to do it.

Feedback isn't always enough, but since it's often neglected, using it could well give you a competitive advantage.

CONSTRUCTIVE CRITICISM

This is when **someone has a definite opinion on your work or performance, and expresses it in a way that is helpful**. It can take the form of either helpful advice (telling you what to do next), or just an insightful critique (in which case you work out what to do next).

Constructive criticism can be either positive or negative, that is the critic may either like or dislike your work, and offer either praise or suggestions for improvement.

Here are some of the characteristics of constructive criticism:

- **PERSPECTIVE**—the critic makes their own viewpoint clear, without claiming to be all knowing.
- **SPECIFIC**—the criticism is detailed enough to make it clear *exactly* what the critic is talking about, and what criteria they are using for judgment.
- **EXAMPLES**—the critic backs up their judgment with specific examples.
- **RELEVANT**—the critic focuses on the most pertinent aspects of the work.
- **NUANCED**—the critic recognizes that performance can be measured in fine gradations, and that there may be alternative ways of evaluating it.
- **RESPECTFUL**—the criticism is not personal and there is no implication that you are a bad performer. The critic talks about you in a way that implies you have the ability to make any necessary improvements.

Whether constructive criticism is encouraging or discouraging is up to you. Of course you are likely to feel encouraged when someone offers you praise. But even if a constructive critique exposes multiple errors and flaws, I'd suggest you shouldn't feel discouraged (even if you don't feel over the moon).

If it's genuinely constructive, then it presents you with an opportunity to fix the problems and improve. I can think of a few times when a critic has respectfully but thoroughly 'shredded' my work, and I have left the room excited to explore the new possibilities they have shown me.

One of your career goals should be to find good sources of constructive criticism. Like feedback, it will give you an advantage—especially over all the people who are too precious to expose themselves to any kind of criticism.

DESTRUCTIVE CRITICISM

This is when **someone has a definite opinion, but either they don't know what they're talking about, or they don't know how to express it properly—or both.**

I call it destructive because of its effect: if you're not careful, it can seriously dent your motivation, your creativity, and your ability to learn. It would be just as accurate to call it **incompetent criticism**, since it reveals more about the critic's failings than the performer's. If criticism is an art, incompetent critics are the ones who can barely draw a stick man.

Here are the typical characteristics of destructive criticism:

- **LACK OF PERSPECTIVE**—the critic speaks as though he or she is the ultimate authority, rather than a human being with a limited viewpoint.
- **VAGUE**—the work is dismissed in general terms ('awful,' 'terrible,' 'no good') without specifying what criteria the judgment is based on.

- **NO EXAMPLES**—the critic fails to back up their judgment with specific examples.
- **IRRELEVANT**—the critic introduces irrelevant criteria, or focuses on an irrelevant aspect of the work.
- **EXAGGERATED**—sweeping, black-and-white judgments, with no acknowledgment of fine grades of quality, or alternative points of view.
- **DISRESPECTFUL**—the critic is rude, aggressive, or otherwise insensitive to the performer's feelings.

If the incompetent critic is a reviewer, heckler, or internet troll, you may decide to just ignore them. If it's a boss or a client, you have a problem—see Chapter 37 on how to deal with them.

PERSONAL ABUSE

Personal abuse is when **somebody makes negative or insulting comments about you personally, with malicious intent**. It should not be confused with criticism.

People who resort to personal abuse tend to do it out of ignorance, prejudice, or because they have 'lost the argument' and realize they can't get at you via legitimate criticism, but it generally doesn't help much to know this.

We'll look at how to deal with personal abuse in Chapter 35 and Chapter 36.

YOUR NEXT STEPS

Next time someone offers you some 'criticism,' ask yourself which of the four categories it fits into:

1. Feedback
2. Constructive criticism
3. Destructive criticism
4. Personal abuse

Then go to the relevant step below for how to deal with it.

1. FEEDBACK

Welcome it. Not only that, you should actively seek out sources of accurate feedback, such as:

- Measuring and recording key data.
- Recording yourself on video.
- Working with a good teacher or coach.

Make time to consider the feedback and ask yourself what you can learn from it.

You can also give yourself feedback, by asking yourself the following questions when you finish a performance or piece of work:

- What specific things did I do well?
- How can I maintain that in future?
- What specific things didn't I do so well?
- How can I fix that in future?

2. CONSTRUCTIVE CRITICISM

As with feedback, you should actively look for people who can give you informed and constructive criticism.

Learn to recognize the characteristics of constructive criticism. Whenever you encounter genuinely constructive criticism (positive or negative) ask yourself what you can learn from it.

When receiving constructive criticism in person, engage with the critic, by asking them to explain anything that isn't clear, and letting them know how much you value their critique and what (if anything) you are going to do with it.

3. DESTRUCTIVE CRITICISM

If destructive criticism comes from someone who isn't directly involved in your work, ignore it.

If it comes from someone who is involved (e.g. a teacher, client, or boss), talk to them and get them to clarify their criticism. I'll explain how to do this in Chapter 37.

4. PERSONAL ABUSE

See Chapter 35 and Chapter 36 for advice on dealing with this.

CHAPTER 25

Why we get criticism out of proportion

"Too long."

"Too many updates."

"Too many words."

"Not as insightful as Seth Godin."

"Boooring!"

"Not enough practical tips for succeeding as a problogger."

These are some of the messages I've received as reasons for unsubscribing to my blog. Compared to the thousands of people who have signed up and stayed happily subscribed for years, the proportion of unsubscribers and messages like this is tiny.

Similarly, the overwhelming majority of comments and emails I receive in response to my blog articles are positive and enthusiastic, expressing agreement or gratitude. Even when people disagree they usually do so politely and respectfully. The rude and nasty ones are very much the exception to the rule.

But it doesn't always feel like that. If I'm not alert, a nasty comment can spoil a morning. I'll turn it over and over in my head, wondering what they meant, why they had to be so rude, or what planet they are living on (or maybe all three).

This can happen even when the criticism is absurd. I once got the 'too many updates' feedback after sending out my first blog post for six months! I don't blog about succeeding as a problogger, nor advertize my blog as offering 'practical tips for succeeding as a problogger,' so that person was obviously in the wrong place.

Why do we get criticism out of proportion like this?

Negativity bias is a well-established principle in psychology, which means humans typically focus more on negative information (such as bad memories and threats) than positive information (such as good memories or opportunities). It's easy to explain hypersensitivity to threats as a survival mechanism with evolutionary benefits: if our ancestors had taken a more relaxed attitude to growling noises in the bushes, they would not have survived long enough to become our ancestors. These days the threats are thankfully verbal rather than physical for most of us, but as we saw in Chapter 3, the threat of social exclusion can feel like a matter of life or death for human beings.

So first up, recognize that getting criticism out of proportion is *normal behavior*, a quirk or side effect of the way we've evolved. Don't beat yourself up for it. And don't make it worse by criticizing yourself for getting it out of proportion! You're only human, and this is what humans tend to do—but there are alternatives…

YOUR NEXT STEPS

1. Next time someone criticizes you, notice how you respond. Try to step back from the situation and look at it more objectively. Do you feel worse than you logically should?

If you struggle to do this, relay the criticism to a friend or trusted colleague and ask them how seriously *they* think you should take it.

2. If you conclude you have a tendency to get criticism out of proportion, start giving yourself the benefit of the doubt: whenever

you catch yourself feeling terrible about a piece of criticism, tell yourself, "I'm overreacting again. It's probably NOT as bad as I assume."

It may take a while before you take this alternative perspective seriously, but keep practicing and notice what difference it makes.

150

CHAPTER 26

How to turn criticism into a crisis

If you don't know how to deal with it, your negativity bias can turn criticism into something that feels like a complete disaster.

The critic's words feel like the confirmation of your worst fears—you were kidding yourself all along, you were stupid to believe otherwise, and you are, in fact a complete and utter failure. Forget just spoiling your day—it feels as though the critic is bringing the curtain down on your entire career. You carry their words around in your head, repeating them and elaborating on their implications, getting more and more anxious and depressed with each repetition.

If that sounds like a familiar experience, read through this chapter to see what you are doing to get the criticism out of proportion—and what to start doing instead, to give yourself a break.

1. ASSUME THE CRITIC IS RIGHT

Because we have evolved to be on high alert for threats, it's easy to take criticism at face value, as an authoritative judgment on our work. If you do this with every piece of criticism that comes your way, you are *guaranteed* to feel terrible.

WHAT TO DO INSTEAD

Adopt an attitude of healthy skepticism to criticism. Don't dismiss it, but don't take it at face value. Recognize that it is bound to sting at first, but try not to take your emotional reaction 100% seriously. Give it a little time, then come back to the criticism and analyze it to see whether or not it has any merit.

2. MULTIPLY THE CRITIC

In Queen's famous video for 'Bohemian Rhapsody', there's a sequence where the four faces of the band members are multiplied into a huge chorus, using state-of-the-art (for 1975) special effects. If you really want to make yourself feel miserable, simply apply the 'Bohemian Rhapsody effect' to multiply the image of the critic in your mind's eye—so that it's not just one person criticizing you, but tens, hundreds, or thousands of people chorusing the criticism (guitar solo optional).

WHAT TO DO INSTEAD

Remind yourself that this is just the opinion of one person, at one time, in one place. There are plenty of others out there who could have a completely different view of your work.

3. TAKE IT PERSONALLY

We've been here before. By now you should recognize the pattern—taking the criticism as a judgment on you as a person; telling yourself it just goes to show you're not a real artist/leader/whatever; and visualizing your future career cleaning toilets and making tea for the people who are really up to the job and not just kidding themselves. And so on...

WHAT TO DO INSTEAD

Focus on the specific aspects of your work or performance that are being criticized.

Does the critic have a point about *these particular instances*? (And remember, if the criticism doesn't include specific examples, that's a sure sign of an incompetent critic.)

Tell yourself that even if you have performed badly in this particular instance, it doesn't mean you are incapable of doing brilliant work in the future.

4. ARGUE WITH THE CRITIC IN YOUR HEAD

This one's a doozy. You imagine having a conversation with the critic, in which you argue back and defend yourself. The trouble is, the critic isn't convinced, and you imagine their response to your defense—and so on, back and forth in your imagination, for hours or even days. It's an exquisite way of torturing yourself, since you get to carry the critic around with you wherever you go, poisoning every aspect of your daily life.

WHAT TO DO INSTEAD

Wake up!

The conversation is not real. It's not happening. Drop it and forget it. Look around you. Breathe fresh air. Go for a walk or run, or coffee with a friend—on the strict condition that you don't mention the critic once!

Make time to process the criticism and decide what to do with it. Then get on with your life.

5. CALL YOURSELF STUPID FOR EVEN TRYING

One part criticism with two parts regret and recrimination is a powerful cocktail. In this scenario, not only do you get to feel bad about the criticism itself, you tell yourself you were stupid to even dream of succeeding. Who did you think you were? How dumb was that? And so on.

WHAT TO DO INSTEAD

Imagine an alternative universe where you never took any risks, never dared to dream big, never made any effort to do anything original, never put yourself on the line in pursuit of your ambitions.

How stupid would *that* be?

Exactly!

But you didn't do that. You stood up to be counted, and were brave enough to expose yourself to criticism for the sake of your dreams. Therefore, you are not stupid. Even if your work was utterly terrible on this occasion, it was still worth doing, if only for the learning (and a juicy anecdote for your autobiography).

6. LET IT FESTER

This is when you don't do anything in particular with the criticism, but it festers at the back of your mind, like an old sack of potatoes at the back of your grocery cupboard. And just like potatoes, the longer you leave it there, the worse it gets. You may not be aware of it consciously, but the smell infiltrates the background of your life, and not in a good way.

In hypnosis, an 'open loop' is when the hypnotist starts telling a story or opening up a topic of conversation, and then leaves it hanging, without a conclusion. The result is that part of your unconscious mind is left waiting for a resolution, which produces a mild trance state.

The more open loops you have in your mental experience, the more your mind becomes enveloped in trance, and the harder it is to wake up and bring your full attention to your present experience. Which is fine if you trust the hypnotist and they bring you out of the trance at the end! It's not so good if the trances consist of criticisms, resentments, arguments, and other unfinished business. That kind of trance, you can do without.

WHAT TO DO INSTEAD

Close the loop. Process the criticism and come out of your trance. 155
Open your eyes and wake up.

156

CHAPTER 27

Get some perspective

As we saw right back in Chapter 3, if you care about your work, you identify with it—so it's inevitable that criticism will hurt. But you don't have to experience agony every time you receive a negative review or a suggestion for improvement. 'No pain no gain' is true up to a point, but if you're blinded by pain you won't gain very much.

157

You will never look at your own work with complete objectivity, but here are four ways you can distance yourself from it, to get criticism in perspective and make better use of it.

1. DISTANCE IN SPACE

Here are some practical tips from Leonardo da Vinci's advice to artists in his *Notebooks*:

> We know very well that errors are better recognized in the works of others than in our own; and that often, while reproving little faults in others, you may ignore great ones in yourself... I say that when you paint you should have a flat mirror and often look at your work as reflected in it, when you will see it reversed, and it will appear to you like some other painter's work, so you will be better able to judge of its faults than in any other way. Again, it is well that you should often leave off work and take a little relaxation, because, when you

come back to it you are a better judge; for sitting too close at work may greatly deceive you. Again, it is good to retire to a distance because the work looks smaller and your eye takes in more of it at a glance and sees more easily the discords or disproportion in the limbs and colors of the objects.

This is great advice for artists and designers, but even a writer like me can benefit from a modified version. If I'm stuck on a piece of writing, I translate it into a different format: I'll take a handwritten draft and type it up on the computer; or if I've been working on the computer, I'll print it out and look at it in the next room. This helps me see the text with fresh eyes, as Leonardo says, as if I were looking at the work of another writer.

Video is a terrific tool for stage and sports performers, showing you things about your movements you could never see otherwise. The same goes for audio recordings for musicians, singers, and speakers.

Sometimes it helps to change the environment where you experience the work. In the film *24 Hour Party People*, the members of Joy Division sit in Tony Wilson's car to listen to their album for the first time, because this is how their audience will hear the songs on the radio.

2. DISTANCE IN TIME

As well as physical distance from the picture, Leonardo suggests that the artist take a break in order to come back better able to judge. Even a short interval can be enough to break the connection with your work and approach it afresh. Many writers follow a similar pattern, setting aside separate times for drafting and revising their text. Here's Maya Angelou describing her writing routine:

If April is the cruellest month, then eight o'clock at night is the cruellest hour, because that's when I start to edit and all that pretty stuff I've written gets axed out. So if I've written 10 or 12 pages in six hours, it'll end up as three or four if I'm lucky.

I always try to finish a piece of writing at least one day before I'm due to submit or publish it—I call this 'letting it marinade.' When I read through it after a break I invariably find several things to tweak that I couldn't see before. By allowing yourself more time to review and revise your work, you sharpen your critical faculty and improve the work.

And when you receive a stinging critique, try not to let your first reaction be your final one. In the heat of the moment you are not the best judge of the criticism. So make an effort to return to it a few days later, and ask yourself—honestly—whether the critic had a point.

3. SEEING THROUGH OTHERS' EYES

The easiest way to find out how your work looks to others is to ask them. Make sure you pick people whose opinion is informed and relevant and who won't spare your feelings.

I attend Mimi Khalvati's poetry workshop because she has an almost supernatural ability to see to the heart of a poem, even in early draft form, and suggest unexpected ways of improving it. She doesn't hold back if the writing isn't up to scratch, but she does it so skillfully that even if she's telling me to rewrite the whole thing I come out of the class eager to get back to work.

If you can find a teacher as good as Mimi, pay plenty of attention to their words. In a work situation, your boss, colleagues, and customers are obvious people to ask. If you're a performer of any kind, you probably won't need to ask, as there will always be plenty of people on the sidelines who are eager to tell you what they think of you!

If you aren't able to ask someone else for real, the next best thing is to use your imagination. Put yourself in their shoes and notice how the world looks through their eyes. Imagine the kind of things they are likely to say.

Try to get at least two different perspectives on your work (in addition to your own).

4. MENTAL DISTANCE

What you're really trying to achieve with all these techniques is to create **mental distance** between yourself, the work, the criticism, and your reaction.

Remember your mindfulness practice?

I keep coming back to it because it's helpful in many different ways. In this case it can help you see the criticism for what it is, get it in perspective and—eventually—let it go.

Hold the criticism and your response to it in your attention—without trying to avoid it, or put it out of your mind. And without exaggerating it or feeding it by arguing with it. While you're doing this, focus on your body, your breathing, and your surroundings. Keep doing this until you start to 'see round the edges' of the criticism—and beyond it.

NOTES

Leonardo da Vinci, "Of judging your own pictures," *Notebooks*, section 530, Project Gutenberg translation: lateralaction.com/leonardo

"A Day in the Life of Maya Angelou," interview by Carol Sarler, *The Sunday Times Magazine*, 27 December 1987

Mimi Khalvati: www.mimikhalvati.co.uk

CHAPTER 28

When to ignore the critics

Leonard Cohen is not your typical rock star. Not only does he write slow, melancholic, poetic songs, with a minimalist acoustic accompaniment, he has also spent several years living the reclu-   161
sive life of a Zen monk, a disciple of the teacher Kyozan Joshu Sasaki Roshi.

In an interview, Cohen told the story of being visited by Roshi at the recording studio during the seventies. The music press critics were writing him off as 'an old depressive drone peddling suicide notes.' When the singer asked his teacher what he thought of the music, Roshi replied: "Leonard, you should sing more sad."

While the critics wanted him to tone it down and deliver something more upbeat, Roshi evidently felt Cohen needed to go in the *opposite* direction—to stop holding back, forget about people's expectations, and fully surrender himself to the sadness.

If Cohen had listened to the critics he would have compromised his art and disappointed his fans. No, his work isn't to everyone's taste, but trying to please everyone is a recipe for disaster for an artist. Or for anyone else who wants to do something truly original. No wonder Cohen said this was the best advice he ever received.

You're better off doing nothing than doing something bland. Sometimes it's important—even fun!—to annoy certain people, and have them hate your work. A nice side effect of this kind of criticism is that your fans will love you all the more, and rush to your defense when they see you being attacked.

ACTION CRITICISM VS. FYI CRITICISM

So how do you decide whether to ignore criticism or do something about it? One way is to divide it into **action criticism** and **FYI criticism**.

ACTION CRITICISM

This is from someone who is directly involved in your work, or whose opinion you take seriously—such as a boss, collaborator, client, teacher, or mentor. When they give you feedback, they expect you to do something about it—either for your benefit (in the case of a teacher or mentor) or theirs (a client) or for everyone's (boss/collaborator).

As long as you're in touch with these people, you need to pay close attention to their criticism and respond to it. You don't necessarily have to do what they want, but you need to at least engage them in dialogue.

If you find their criticism helpful (even if it's not always comfortable) let them know. If you don't find their criticism helpful, you have a choice to make—either get them to change (see Chapter 37) or stop working with them.

FYI CRITICISM

'FYI' means 'For Your Information'—no action required. On an email or memo, it lets you know you are not expected to respond, just to read and take note of the contents.

Here I'm using it in a special sense, to refer to criticism from anyone whose opinion you are at liberty to ignore. You don't have a working or teaching relationship with this person. They are a reviewer, academic critic, blogger, commenter on your blog or Facebook page. FYI criticism includes praise and blame—the glowing review as well as the snarky blog comment.

I'm calling it FYI criticism from *your* point of view. Maybe they expect a response, but you don't have to reply. Sometimes they will be rude or aggressive in order to provoke a response—in which case you may feel less like responding.

You don't even have to listen to this kind of criticism. At a certain point in his career, P.G. Wodehouse gave up his cuttings agency—who scoured the press and sent him reviews and other references to him and his work—because he found it a distraction from his writing. Blogger Leo Babauta switched off the popular comments section of his blog at Zenhabits.net for the same reason—to allow him to focus on his writing.

YOUR NEXT STEPS

1.   Next time you receive a piece of criticism, stop and ask yourself whether it's action criticism or FYI criticism.

2.   If it's action criticism, ask yourself whether it's useful. If so, let the critic know and thank them—this makes it more likely they will give you more helpful criticism in future.

If not, try to get them to change their approach (Chapter 37 will help you do this). If they refuse to change, ask yourself whether you really need to work with this person.

3.   If it's FYI criticism and you find it interesting or useful, take what you can from it. If you don't find it useful, ignore it. If it descends into personal abuse, see Chapter 36 for how to deal with it.

If you find yourself being distracted by a lot of unhelpful FYI criticism from one particular source—for example, an online forum or a particular journalist—cut that source out of your life. You have more important things to spend your energy on.

NOTE

Leonard Cohen interview, *Rolling Stone,* Issue 881, November 2001

CHAPTER 29

Who do they think they are?

When you're faced with criticism, it's easy to take it at face value. But as Leonard Cohen's story shows us, **who is talking** is at least as important as what they are saying.

You might not take kindly to an armchair tennis player giving you advice about your backhand, but if the same words came out of the mouth of a grand slam champion, you'd be all ears, however brutal their assessment.

So before deciding what to do about a piece of criticism, always consider where it's coming from. Here are some of the usual sources:

HATERS AND TROLLS

These people get a kick out of making nasty, offensive, and abusive comments. Many of them don't have the guts to criticize you to your face, so they are particularly common on the internet, where they are known as **trolls**. They are a tiny minority, but a vocal one.

It's generally best to ignore them. I've occasionally received an embarrassed apology when I've replied to an abusive comment or email, but most of them aren't interested in dialogue. If they persist see Chapter 36 for how to deal with them.

If it helps, look on it as a positive sign that you're attracting enough attention for the haters to notice you and get annoyed. Trying to avoid upsetting anyone is a recipe for mediocrity.

THE PEANUT GALLERY

This is the term my friend Sonia Simone uses for all the people who have an opinion on your work, but who are irrelevant to your goals. They include the nit-pickers and 'yes-butters' who will always find a flaw in your argument, and the well-intentioned nice people who keep asking you to do something different, even though you're not remotely interested in doing it.

You can safely ignore these people too. Be polite, and make a brief reply if you want to, but don't take them too seriously. And don't get sidetracked into playing their game.

THE PUBLIC

I'm not a fan of Henry James's novels, but even I had to feel sorry for him when I heard that story about him being booed off stage by the public at the premiere of one of his plays. There's no humiliation like a public humiliation.

How seriously you take the public's opinion will depend on what business you're in. If you're the editor of a national newspaper, or commissioning a piece of public art, you will probably pay more attention to it than if you're an avant-garde novelist, or a creator of fine art that only the richest of the rich can afford. If you're in a punk band, it would be downright embarrassing to discover everybody and their grandmother tapping their feet and singing along to your songs.

So forget 'the public' and decide who *your* public is. Once you know who they are, then you can start worrying about what they think of you.

THE PROFESSIONAL CRITICS

These are the people whose job it is to critique the work and careers of performers in their field. Traditionally they have been newspaper reviewers, literary critics, academics, and TV or radio pundits. These days they are just as likely to be bloggers and social media power users.

There are basically two kinds of professional critic: the ones who 'get' what you're trying to do; and the ones who don't. Pay more attention to the former than the latter. And as we saw in the last chapter, the sharper your own critical thinking skills, the more confident you will be in assessing the judgment of professional critics.

But don't be too quick to criticize the critics. Sometimes they tell us just what we need to hear, even if we don't want to hear it.

YOUR PEERS

The obvious thing to watch out for here is rivalry. Are they delivering constructive criticism, or trying to take you down a peg or two? Often it's a bit of both. And maybe that's no bad thing—creative tensions have been at the heart of many artistic partnerships and friendships (Wordsworth and Coleridge, Kahlo and Rivera, Lennon and McCartney).

And remember, there is one thing your peers can offer you that no one else can—the perspective of someone in a situation very similar to yours.

YOUR MENTOR(S)

A mentor is an experienced pro who shares what he or she has learned. Roshi, Yoda, and Mr Miyagi are classic mentors. If you're lucky enough to have a mentor who knows you well enough to make an informed judgment about your work, and who cares enough to tell you where you need to improve, then you owe it to them—and to yourself—to listen.

Tennis player Andy Murray had been teetering on the brink of major tournament success for years, but it was not until he hired veteran champion Ivan Lendl as his coach that he won the Olympic Gold Medal and US Open in quick succession. Murray had the talent and stamina to get within touching distance of a major trophy—but he credited his mentor with helping him reach out and seize it.

Mentors are not infallible, and sometimes you reach the point where you've outgrown them. But it often pays to give them the benefit of the doubt, and consider their criticisms carefully instead of dismissing them. (Just ask Darth Vader.)

YOUR NEXT STEPS

Next time you encounter criticism, ask yourself who is speaking:

- **HATERS AND TROLLS**—ignore them. If that doesn't work, see Chapter 36.
- **THE PEANUT GALLERY**—ignore them. Or be polite but don't take them seriously.
- **THE PUBLIC**—firstly, separate the general public from your public (your fans and/or potential customers). Ignore the former; listen to the latter, even if you don't always do what they want.

- **PROFESSIONAL CRITICS**—firstly, separate the ones who 'get' what you are trying to do from the ones who don't. Feel free to ignore the latter. Analyze the former's words carefully, to see whether there's anything you can learn from them.
- **YOUR PEERS**—firstly, try to distinguish between rivalry and genuine criticism. Secondly, ask yourself whether they have a point, and what you can learn from them.
- **YOUR MENTOR(S)**—listen carefully to what they say and consider it over time. If it's not clear, ask them to explain further. When in doubt, give them the benefit of the doubt.

NOTE

For Sonia Simone's take on the 'peanut gallery' see: www.copyblogger.com/smart-people-peanut-gallery

CHAPTER 30

Your harshest critic

You know who I mean.

Typically, your harshest critic is not the one who gives you a bad review, or leaves a snarky comment online, or heckles during a presentation, or delivers a scathing put-down in a meeting. It's a lot closer to home than that. These critics can only really touch a nerve when they say something you are already saying to yourself.

Or to put it another way, they chime in with your Inner Critic.

If you don't pay attention to what is happening here, you will be at the mercy of your Inner Critic—and the external critics who somehow manage to channel it—for the rest of your life. But if you recognize the presence of your Inner Critic, and find a way of dealing with it, you will become far more resilient.

The most important thing to understand here is that **your Inner Critic is not telling the ultimate truth about you**. It's just a small part of you, giving you a highly selective and distorted account of yourself.

But the Inner Critic is cunning. There is usually a grain of truth in its criticisms, which it uses to convince you of its point of view. And it does this so often, so intimately, and so persistently, that you hardly notice its presence.

Dealing with the Inner Critic is another reason to practice mindfulness every day. When you do this, and you get to know your own thoughts and feelings, you will find it easier to spot the Inner Critic going about its business. And once you see it clearly for what it is, you will find it much harder to take the Inner Critic seriously.

YOUR NEXT STEPS

1.   Keep up your mindfulness practice. (You haven't taken a break already have you?)

2.   Make a list of your harshest critics, and the most painful pieces of criticism you have ever received.
     Read through each criticism in turn, and ask yourself whether your Inner Critic habitually tells you something similar. If so, take heart—you have rumbled the Inner Critic! This is the beginning of the end of its power over you.

3.   Look out for the Inner Critic. Maybe reading through the list is enough to conjure it out of the shadows. Or maybe you'll notice it whispering in your ear the next time you find yourself having a bad day.
     As soon as you notice the Inner Critic, snap into mindfulness: pay attention to your body, your breathing, and your surroundings, while keeping the Critic in your awareness. Don't try to squash the Critic or get rid of it—it will only come back stronger. This is your chance to see through it.
     Do you experience the Critic's thoughts as if you were listening to an inner voice? If so, is it male or female? In your left or right ear?
     Do you have an image of the Critic in your mind's eye? If so, notice its appearance.
     Keep the Critic in your awareness, and notice that it really is just a small part of you. Recognize that what the Critic is saying is not the ultimate truth about you.

3.   You may find it helpful to visualize the Critic as a parrot sitting on your shoulder, jabbering into your ear. Look at it preening itself, puffed up with its own importance. Listen to its squawking voice and notice how hard it is to take the parrot seriously.

4.   Each time the Inner Critic pipes up, stop and ask yourself: "Okay, that's what my worst enemy would say about me. What would my best friend say?"

No, your best friend doesn't always tell you the ultimate truth about yourself either. But calling him or her to mind in response to the Critic will help you maintain a healthier balance.

CRITICISM

CHAPTER 31

Why your Inner Critic is (potentially) your best friend

The Inner Critic gets a lot of bad press, especially among blocked writers and artists who wish the nagging critical voice at the back of their mind would disappear. No wonder there's so much advice on how to banish, silence, or obliterate the Inner Critic. By the time the personal development gurus are done, the Critic's had a tougher pounding than an extra from *Kill Bill*.

(OK, I got you to dress the Critic up in a parrot suit in the last chapter, but notice I didn't tell you to try to get rid of it. Because I know that would be doomed to failure.)

Do you ever wonder why the Critic keeps coming back for more? Could it be that the Critic is actually a very important part of you? One that might even—whisper it—*turn out to be a valuable friend and ally*?

If you think about it, you'd be in big trouble without an Inner Critic. Without some kind of internal quality filter, you'd be happy to churn out any old rubbish and join the ranks of mediocrities. A finely honed critical faculty is one of the things that separates a successful professional from the legions of amateurs.

In the words of musician Mike Monday:

A good producer and a great producer have the same number of ideas—some good, some great. But a great producer will know the difference.

And the great producer's Inner Critic is the difference that makes the difference. Because the great producer has listened more keenly and thought more sharply about music, he or she has a more powerful and useful Inner Critic.

So stop looking at the Inner Critic as the enemy. Try to see it as an over-zealous friend who is delivering criticism too forcefully and without considering your feelings. We all have friends who do that from time to time.

The trick is to get the Critic back 'onside,' delivering genuinely constructive criticism. Like the inspiring mentor who urged you to do your best and didn't accept anything less, but with a supportive and encouraging tone of voice.

CRITICISM AND CREATION ARE NOT MUTUALLY EXCLUSIVE

One of the sacred cows of the creative thinking industry is that we should separate idea generation and evaluation, so that they don't interfere with each other. But my experience as a writer and a coach for hundreds of artists suggests that this isn't how many creative professionals work.

When I'm writing, I'm reading, evaluating, and tweaking as I go. I'll write a few sentences then pause and go back to read them through. Sometimes it's immediately obvious I haven't quite captured the thought or image, so I'll make a few changes before I go on. If I get stuck, I'll stop and read through the whole piece, trying to pick up the thread of inspiration where I lost it. Once

I see where I got tangled up, it's a relief to untangle it and get going again.

For all of this, I have my Inner Critic to thank. And I hear a similar story from many of my coaching clients, who include musicians, designers, filmmakers, fine artists, and all kinds of other creative disciplines—so I'm pretty sure it's not just a writer's thing.

Yes, it's helpful to have designated times when you're *mostly* focused on dreaming up ideas, or tinkering with a prototype, or getting the first draft down as quickly as possible. But the next time you're doing this, you may well notice that you're bringing your sharp critical intelligence into play even at this stage—so you're improving the work even as you create it.

It's also helpful to have dedicated time to review your work, especially toward the end of a project. But even as you critique your work, you'll probably find yourself itching to do some hands-on remodeling or redrafting—calling your freewheeling imagination into play as well. Once again, creation and criticism work hand in hand.

THE INNER CRITIC IS ON YOUR SIDE (REALLY)

So why does the Inner Critic work so hard to tell you the worst possible thing that an audience could say about you and your work?

Partly it's for your own satisfaction—by holding you to high standards, it wants you to achieve the best you can. And believe it or not, it's also trying to *protect* you. By warning you of the potential critiques and humiliations you could experience if you expose your work to the world, it gives you the chance to correct any mistakes.

Or at least to brace yourself for the worst.

No, it's probably not doing it very tactfully or effectively. But the tips below will help you nudge it in the right direction, and help you begin a different kind of relationship with your Inner Critic.

YOUR NEXT STEPS

Here are some suggestions for making better use of your Inner Critic. Experiment with one or two of them at a time, to see what works best for you.

1.   Take a few moments to reflect on the advantages of having a finely honed critical faculty, such as understanding what makes a good piece of work, knowing how to assess your own work and improve it. Sometimes this kind of appreciation is all it takes to get the Critic to quieten down.

2.   You may find it helpful to use one workspace for drafting/sketching/experimenting/rehearsing, and another for reviewing your work.

3.   When you're working, if the Critic starts telling you what's wrong with the piece, ask yourself, "So what does the work need *instead*?" or, "So what do I need to do to make it better?"

4.   If the Critic keeps interfering, promise yourself that you'll do a critical review at the end of this stage of the project—this way you can afford to ignore it for now and keep your momentum going. And make sure you keep your promise! Otherwise the Critic will feel the need to keep interrupting.

5.   Make time to review your work. Get into the habit of doing this before you hit 'publish' or send off your work, or step onto

the stage or games pitch. The more consistently and effectively you do this, the more the Critic will relax and let you get on with things in the early stages.

6.   Imagine sitting down for a coffee with your Inner Critic. Thank it for its good intentions—holding you to high standards, and warning you about potential criticisms from others. Then gently but firmly let it know that the way it's delivering its criticism isn't very helpful.

Run through the characteristics of destructive criticism, and ask it to stop using this approach:

- **LACK OF PERSPECTIVE**—the Critic speaks as though he or she is the ultimate authority.
- **VAGUE**—the work is dismissed in general terms ('awful,' 'terrible,' 'no good') without specifying what criteria the judgment is based on.
- **NO EXAMPLES**—the Critic fails to back up their judgment with specific examples.
- **IRRELEVANT**—the Critic introduces irrelevant criteria, or focuses on an irrelevant aspect of the work.
- **EXAGGERATED**—sweeping, black-and-white judgments, with no acknowledgment of fine grades of quality, or alternative points of view.
- **DISRESPECTFUL**—the Critic is rude, aggressive, or otherwise insensitive to your feelings.

And start using the principles of constructive criticism instead:

- **PERSPECTIVE**—the Critic makes his or her viewpoint clear, without claiming to be all knowing.

- **SPECIFIC**—the criticism is detailed enough to make it clear *exactly* what the Critic is talking about, and what criteria they are using for judgment.
- **EXAMPLES**—the Critic backs up their judgment with specific examples.
- **RELEVANT**—the Critic focuses on the most pertinent aspects of the work.
- **NUANCED**—the Critic recognizes that performance can be measured in fine gradations, and that there may be alternative ways of evaluating it.
- **RESPECTFUL**—the criticism is not personal and there is no implication that you are a bad performer. The Critic talks about you in a way that implies you have the ability to make any necessary improvements.

NOTE

A version of this chapter was first published online at 99u.com

CHAPTER 32

Eight ways to sharpen your critical thinking skills

Supposing you had never learned to ice skate or to play hockey.
You would be taking your life in your hands if you took part in
an ice hockey match between two teams of hardened professionals. It's the same with criticism: if you've never developed your
own critical thinking skills, you are likely to emerge bruised and
battered from a clash with a professional critic or internet troll.

But if you spend a bit of time beefing up your own critical
faculty, you will be a lot more confident of handling yourself in
a fight. When you learn to recognize excellence, and understand
why you prefer one type of excellence over another, you will become more discerning about your own work and more confident
in your tastes.

Here are eight different approaches to sharpening your critical
thinking, and having some fun in the process.

1. GET TO KNOW YOUR FIELD INSIDE-OUT

This isn't about knowing everything it's possible to know about
your industry, art form, sport, or whatever. That's unnecessary
as well as impossible. What you need is to first decide on the

boundaries of your field of expertise, and then to make yourself an expert on everything *inside* those boundaries.

I remember the day I gave up trying to be 'well read' in the conventional sense. Having studied for an English degree, I felt a familiar twinge of anxiety when somebody mentioned a classic work of literature that I had never read. Given how many classic works of literature have been written over the centuries, and the time it would take to read them all, the odds of freeing myself from this anxiety in this lifetime felt depressingly slim.

So I gave up.

I resolved never to be anxious or embarrassed to tell anyone—including you—that I have never read a novel by Jane Austen, or come to think of it, by Thackeray, Dickens, Balzac, or Dostoevsky. I'm sure they are all wonderful writers, and one day I may get round to reading some of them, but only if I really want to. Life's too short to spend it working through someone else's reading list.

But poetry is a different matter. I love reading poetry and I want to get better at writing it, so I intend to read as much of it as possible for the rest of my life. At the moment, I'm filling in some of the gaps in my knowledge of 20th-century American poetry, not out of a misguided sense of completeness, but because it's wonderful stuff and life's too short to miss it. I'll never read all the great poetry that has ever been written, but that's a good thing, as it means there will always be more for me to discover.

You can do the same. Decide on your desired field of expertise—make it wide enough to be inexhaustible, but narrow enough to be manageable.

Now make a list of the major players/works within your chosen field, and start working your way through it—reading the books, watching/listening to the recordings, and so on. Don't skip the ones you don't like! Get to know them, and understand why others like them even if you don't.

2. READ REVIEWS WITH A CRITICAL EYE

Reviews in mainstream publications are often treated with reverence, as if they represented the gospel truth about a new piece of work. But have you ever noticed how badly written some of them are? How poorly constructed the argument is? How obvious their biases are? And how little evidence they produce to back up their assertions?

One of my pet hates is seeing a poetry review in which the reviewer hasn't bothered to quote a single line of verse. It's hard to take someone seriously who does this, yet I've seen it happen in respected journals.

Never take reviews at face value. Read them with a critical eye, asking yourself:

- What do you agree with?
- What do you disagree with?
- What is questionable (even if you agree)?
- What is the critic's bias?
- What did the critic leave out?

Sharpen your skills further by writing an alternative review, with a different take on the work. You earn bonus points for publishing it on your blog or placing it in a magazine!

3. READ CRITICS AND PRACTITIONERS

I'm not wild about academic poetry criticism, with a few exceptions. I'm much more interested in essays, criticism, and interviews by practicing poets. Until you've tried to do something yourself, you never really appreciate how difficult it is, so insights from people who have done it at the highest level are like gold dust.

Get to know the main critics in your field, and familiarize yourself with their opinions. And find out everything you can about what the outstanding practitioners have said about their work. Read their books, articles, and interviews, watch documentaries about them, and read their (auto)biographies. Compile a collection of particularly inspiring quotations.

4. DEBATE WITH FRIENDS

Spend time with friends who share your passion, even if—especially if—they strongly disagree with you on some topics. Debate with them. Challenge each other's assumptions, and make each other justify every statement, backing it up with solid evidence and a coherent argument. Just don't take anything too seriously after the second drink!

5. JOIN A GROUP (OR START ONE)

Find a class, workshop, or discussion group, where like-minded enthusiasts gather to sharpen each other's minds. (Remember MeetUp.com is a good place to look for these.)

If there isn't a group like this in your area, start one. It could be as informal as a monthly meeting in the pub, or as ambitious as weekly screenings of Kurosawa's entire film catalogue. Maybe everyone has to write something every week, or one person has to give a presentation to kick off the discussion.

And make sure most people in the room know more than you do. If you feel slightly intimidated by others' knowledge, but excited to learn from them, you'll know you're in the right place.

6. CONTRIBUTE TO A FORUM

Search on the web for forums. Other places to look include groups on social networks such as Facebook or LinkedIn. If you're lucky, you'll strike gold—a busy, well established community hosting daily in-depth discussions on topics that fascinate you, populated by friendly obsessives who seem to spend several hours a day on the site. Welcome to your virtual village.

Start off by reading through the discussion threads to tune into the conversation, then introduce yourself and join in. If you've found a good forum, it is a marvelous opportunity to share your thinking, debate topics, and examine your own assumptions in a respectful and supportive atmosphere. (Just beware of spending all day on there.)

7. START A BLOG

If you really want to work out what you really think about a topic, and put your ideas out there to see what the world makes of them, there's nothing quite like blogging. Knowing that anyone could drop by your site and leave a comment, or write a counter-argument on their own site is a great way to focus your mind. It forces you to consider other people's opinions, and how they relate to your own. It's a great confidence-booster when readers let you know they appreciate your words.

One of the great benefits of blogging is the way it exposes you to potential criticism and inoculates you to it. Don't let the fear put you off. Before I started my first blog, I had visions of snarky commenters and condescending uber-bloggers tearing my ideas to shreds. But I really wanted to try. And I've been overwhelmed by how much positive, supportive, and enthusiastic feedback I've received. Experiencing such a great response online has encouraged me to speak up and put my ideas out there in other places.

8. BENCHMARK AGAINST THE BEST

Sometimes even excellence can be pretty mediocre.

Right now, in your field, there are people who are revered as stars. People hang on their every word, and their projects are launched with great fanfare. But are they *really* that good? Does their work *really* stack up against the best that has ever been done? Or are they merely the best of the current crop? Could it be that there are other contemporaries who don't attract the same notice, yet whose work may be even better than the ones whose names are on everybody's lips? Unless you have a finely developed critical judgment of your own, it's hard to tell.

The same goes for your own work.

One of the dangers of being 'pretty good' at something is complacency. If you're better than everyone else around you, where's your incentive to improve?

- If you're the star player on the team, isn't it time you found a better team?
- If you can run your department with your eyes closed, isn't it time you looked for a challenge that keeps you awake at night?
- If your writing is good enough to be published, is it good enough to be published (and read) in 500 years' time?
- If you've had a hit record, how would you feel about playing it to the music legend who is your hero, and hearing their honest opinion of it?

Whether evaluating other people's work or your own, it makes a big difference what you take as your benchmark. If you measure the work against local or contemporary standards, it's a lot easier to be impressed (by others) or proud (of yourself). But if you're a basketball player it's sobering to compare your stats to those of Michael Jordan. A Man Booker Prize may be nice, but how does your novel stack up against Tolstoy? It's great to have a thriving business, but how does yours compare to Richard Branson's?

If those sound like unfair comparisons, what does that tell you about the assumptions you're making? Or about the kind of ceiling you are placing on your ambition? What difference would it make if you challenged those assumptions, smashed the ceiling, and aimed higher?

Look at a piece of work that's currently in vogue, and measure it against the very highest standards (including 'greats' from the past):

- Does it have the same ambition?
- The same technical demands?
- The same level of execution?
- Comparable originality?
- Similar impact?

Do the same with your own work from time to time.

CHAPTER 33

Criteria (part one)—What game are you playing?

One of my enduring memories of school is the outdoor playground—a huge tarmac space under a gunmetal sky, with pupils in black and gray uniforms running in all directions.

The only colors I remember are the criss-crossed markings for different sports—tennis, badminton, football (the soccer kind), basketball, netball—painted on the tarmac. They were all overlaid on top of each other, which would have been horrendously confusing, if they hadn't been different colors—yellow for tennis, red for football, orange for basketball, and so on.

We didn't give it a second thought at the time, but the first thing we had to do before we started playing was to adjust our vision to the markings of that particular game. Like a Magic Eye illusion, if you were playing football, those red lines had to pop out at you. Your ability to play to them was critical once the game started. It made all the difference to how hard you hit a pass, whether it was worth sprinting to keep the ball in play, and whether the goalie had handled the ball outside the area. Play to the wrong line for an instant and you could lose the game.

Even within the markings of individual sports there were variations, such as the different boundaries for singles and doubles tennis. In football, it was usually agreed that the goalkeeper wasn't allowed to leave the penalty area—but were outfield players allowed to *enter* it? And were we playing the rule that meant attackers were only allowed to shoot once they had crossed a certain line? These questions had to be settled before the whistle blew to start the game.

Obviously there would have been chaos and arguments if one team started playing basketball while the other began playing football. The players would have had different goals in mind, and their strategies and tactics would have been completely out of sync. Fair play to one team would be an obvious foul to the other. If you're going to play together, you need to agree on the rules of the game you're playing.

This is blindingly obvious when it comes to sports. But in other spheres, it's amazing how often human beings start collaborating, competing, and judging each other *without any clear agreement about exactly what game they are playing, what the rules are, and what success or failure looks like.* Everyone is playing a different game, so it's no wonder there are arguments, disappointments, and recriminations.

Whenever you work on a project or compete for an opportunity, one of the first things you need to know is: **what are the criteria for success?**

Criteria are like the markings on the playground—reference points that mark out the field of endeavor, indicating what is and isn't acceptable, and how success is defined. They don't predetermine the outcome, but they narrow the options.

Once you understand how criteria work, a lot of confusing and frustrating conversations will make more sense. And it will be a lot easier to understand and deal with the criticism that comes your way.

In poetry, for example, for the last hundred years or so there has been an ongoing debate about the merits of traditional verse forms (with regular meter, rhyme, and so on) versus 'free verse' (with no established patterns for such things). One well-known criticism of free verse is that it's 'like playing tennis with the net down,' that is, too easy to be worth doing. On the other hand, some advocates of free verse describe formal verse as a 'straitjacket' that constricts poets' freedom of expression.

With our 'criteria goggles' on, we can see that 'difficulty' is a positive criterion for some traditionalists, whereas 'freedom' is more appealing to those on the free verse side (as the name suggests). So it's perfectly possible for two poetry enthusiasts to have a completely different assessment of the merits of a poet's work, depending which side of the fence they are on.

Personally I enjoy both types, even if my own verse tends towards traditional forms. And it's not just an academic distinction. If I'm in a workshop and someone criticizes my sonnet for using an 'old-fashioned' verse form, then I know they aren't interested in the game I'm playing, and we'll have to agree to disagree. But if they make suggestions about my handling of the form, and point out some ways I could improve on it, I'll be interested in their critique.

Supposing Max, an engineer, goes for a job interview. Before the interview, he spends a lot of time boning up on his technical knowledge, anxious to demonstrate how much he knows. During the interview he talks at length about the technical parameters of a proposed project. In his enthusiasm he even contradicts one of the interviewers and argues that they are going about things the wrong way. He's confident that he's won the argument and demonstrates his expertise. But he doesn't realize the interviewers are keen to recruit a team player with excellent communication skills, who will put colleagues and clients at ease. Knowledge is an important criterion for them, but (as they said in the job spec) "the successful candidate will also have excellent communication skills."

So whether you're talking about poetry, a job interview, or any other kind of performance, the key questions to answer right at the beginning are:

- What game are we playing?
- What are the rules and conventions?
- What are the criteria for success?

You should also ask these questions whenever you're on the receiving end of criticism. Knowing the critic's criteria will help you decide how relevant and useful it is and what to do with it.

Depending on the context, you can get the answers to these questions in several ways...

Sometimes the critic will spell out their criteria. They'll say things like:

- "Needs to work on her technical skills." (Criterion: technical ability.)
- "A promising plot, spoiled by wooden characterization and stilted dialogue." (Criteria: well-structured plot, convincing characterization and realistic dialogue.)
- "Great vision, but the numbers don't add up." (Criterion: value for money or profitability.)
- "The team was well-organized in defense, but they lacked the attacking flair to create opportunities." (Criteria: organization and creativity.)

If you're in communication with the critic, you can ask them or challenge them to spell out their criteria.

If they don't spell them out, or if you don't have the chance to ask, you may be able to reverse-engineer their criteria, by looking at the kind of work or people they have approved in the past.

If you are pushing the boundaries of conceptual art installations, and you receive a withering critique from a specialist in 18th century landscape paintings, you probably shouldn't lose too much sleep. You may even take it as a compliment!

Once you've established a critic's criteria, you know what game they are playing. But is that the game you want to play? Or are you trying to do something entirely different? Your answers will tell you a lot about the kind of opportunities you should pursue, and the kind of critics you should pay attention to along the way.

YOUR NEXT STEPS

1. Next time someone criticizes you or your work, start by trying to identify their criteria.

   Do they spell the criteria out? *If so, go to step 3.*

   Or is their criticism vague and general? *If so, clarify it at step 2.*

2. If they give you vague or general feedback, and you get the opportunity, ask for clarification:

   - What specifically did you do or not do that led to their negative judgment?
   - What specific behaviors were they looking for that you did not demonstrate?
   - What specific characteristics of the work failed to meet their approval?

3. Once you understand their criteria, ask yourself whether you share them? Is this a game you want to play?

   If so, the next chapter will help you get better at playing it.

   If not and it's FYI criticism: what kind of game do you want to play? Who is playing that game? Look for fellow performers as well as critics and gatekeepers who share your criteria, and look for opportunities to connect with them.

   If not, and it's action criticism, you need to negotiate with the critic—see Chapter 37.

CHAPTER 34

Criteria (part two)—How good are you?

Once you find a game worth playing, you naturally want to become a better player. This is where understanding criteria can
give you a competitive edge. When you know the critical factors
in evaluating performance, you can use these as springboards
for improvement.

Criteria are most useful when they help you formulate **specific, concrete examples of what 'better' looks like**. Otherwise
it's like playing on a pitch with no markings or goals, where you
are more likely to succeed by luck than judgment.

Here are some suggestions on how to clarify your criteria for
success, at **basic**, **intermediate**, and **advanced** levels.

1. PROCESS (BASIC)

For process-oriented tasks, where there is a clear right and wrong
way to do things, it's relatively easy to come up with specific examples of successful performance. Health and Safety drills, proofreading guidelines, and driving lessons are designed with this
purpose in mind.

Many forms of martial arts include *kata*—literally 'form'—sets of
prescribed movements to be performed in sequence, such as a series
of attacks and defenses. Kata are tightly choreographed in order

to teach correct posture and movement. There's no room for creativity. Students spend hours practicing the movements, using demonstrations, video, and feedback from instructors to guide them.

At the level of process there should be plenty of instructions available, so make the most of them. But if you're really on the path to achieving something remarkable, you're not going to do it by just following instructions.

2. TECHNIQUE (INTERMEDIATE)

The next level involves tasks that are performed according to principles rather than rigid rules. Things like public speaking, tennis strokes, baseball pitching, plotting a novel, using perspective in painting, or meter and rhyme in poetry. Sooner or later, you'll need to develop your own style, and maybe do things in an original way. But familiarizing yourself with tried and tested principles can speed up your journey to mastery.

At this intermediate stage, a skilled teacher can be tremendously helpful, giving you very specific feedback about where you're going wrong and practical advice on improving. They can show you how to structure your presentation for maximum impact, or eliminate a distracting gesture. They can tweak the angle of your arm so that you hit or throw the ball with greater speed and precision. They can help you smooth out inconsistencies in your plot. They can give you exercises in perspective or versification to establish the principles firmly in your mind.

Criteria are useful here since they help you focus on the specific elements you need to improve. In the examples above, we can identify **structure**, **body language**, **speed**, **precision**, and **formal technique** as the key criteria. Once you know these criteria, it's relatively straightforward to identify good examples and measure yourself against them.

For example, if you delivered a rambling, incoherent presentation, a teacher could give you an example of a really well-structured talk, explain how it differs from yours, and show you how to use the same principles to structure your own talk. In this scenario you'd spend more time with your laptop than on the podium. But if your structure was good but your body language let you down, then you'd spend more time watching videos or live demonstrations, and practicing your delivery.

No, technique is not enough for artistry. But I've noticed that real artists tend to have a healthier respect for technique than the amateurs who dismiss it as 'not the real thing.' As Banksy famously said, "All artists are willing to suffer for their work. But why are so few prepared to learn to draw?"

3. MASTERY (ADVANCED)

When you move beyond technique towards mastery, it's down to you to figure out what to do next. When it comes to jazz improvisation, mazy runs on the football pitch, or leading a team through a crisis, nobody can tell you the 'right answer,' because there isn't one.

At this stage, teachers and critics are there to raise your awareness of your own performance, as a prompt to your own creativity. You will get more from a critic who helps you see a habitual weakness, or a coach who asks you probing questions, than from an instructor who tries to tell you what to do.

The better you get, the more people will be telling you how wonderful you are, which is nice, but dangerous. If you only hear the praise, it's hard to know how to improve. So find critics with sufficient insight and experience to hold you to higher standards. They could be professional reviewers, academics, a mentor, a friend, or even a rival. And ultimately, you need to learn how to do this for yourself—making the transition from being your own worst critic to your own best critic.

Among the many criteria you or your critics can invoke at this stage, two are particularly important: **your own standards** and those of **exemplars**.

YOUR OWN STANDARDS

When it comes to **your own standards**, it's invaluable to have at least one critic who knows you well enough to spot when you are true to your own talent and aspirations and when you veer aside, into the easy option, the rehearsed formula, or the crowd-pleasing gesture. Maybe everyone else is showering you with praise, awards, and/or flowers—but the critic speaks up, like the voice of your conscience. And it may be hard to hear the criticism. When everyone else is inflating your ego, it's painful to have someone apply a pin!

But if you look honestly into your heart, you should see whether or not they have a point. And hopefully you will get better at doing this for yourself, without the need for someone else to point it out to you.

EXEMPLARS

Exemplars—people who are shining examples of stellar achievement—become more and more important the better you get. Because there are fewer people in your immediate circle who can match your performance, it's vital to keep your exemplars in mind.

For example, having achieved considerable success in the first part of his career, the poet Seamus Heaney wrote a perceptive article about W.B. Yeats, where he said Yeats was the kind of poet who "bothers you with the suggestion" that once you have mastered one type of poetry, you should try writing a different kind. If Heaney had used poetry prizes or reviews in the *Times Literary*

Supplement as his criteria for success, he might have been tempted to rest on his laurels. But when he looked at the achievement of Yeats, he found he had plenty to learn.

Choose your exemplars with care. Make sure you pick someone whose example genuinely resonates with you. Steve Jobs achieved amazing things in his lifetime, and if you want to build a company as big as Apple, you can learn a lot from his example. But maybe you're not interested in building an empire on that scale. Maybe you'd rather keep your business small, manageable, and meaningful in your own terms. In which case you might be better off taking a leaf out of Derek Sivers' book *Anything You Want*, in which he tells the inspiring story of 'accidentally' growing a $22 million business, while trying to keep it as small as possible.

As well as choosing exemplars from your own field, feel free to take a few from other fields, as this can open up some really creative avenues for you. David Ogilvy modeled his advertising agency on the kitchen of Monsieur Pitard, head chef of the Hotel Majestic in Paris. Supposing you started a company with the aim of doing for business what David Bowie did for rock 'n' roll, you'll probably come up with something more original than the person who wants to be the next Bill Gates.

Once you've chosen your exemplars, don't try to ape their personality, their quirks, or even their methods. Focus on the particular qualities they embody that make your spine tingle — because those are the ones that teach you something about your own nature and potential.

YOUR NEXT STEPS

How to raise your game depends on whether you're working at the level of process, technique, or mastery:

1. PROCESS
Identify exactly where you went wrong, and what the correct procedure is to get it right. Use reference materials—instruction manuals, textbooks, videos—or get an instructor to tell you what to do, and practice until you can do it standing on your head. Memorize essential information.

2. TECHNIQUE
Get as much detailed information as you can about your performance measured according to the key criteria.

If you can, ask the critic these questions:

- What exactly will success look like?
- What specifically am I doing wrong?
- What specifically should I be doing instead?

If you're not able to ask the critic, ask yourself these questions and see what you can come up with. You may want to enlist a teacher to help you with this.

Next, practice and get high-quality feedback—video yourself, get feedback from a coach, take a test—whatever it takes to verify that you are improving.

3. MASTERY
At this level, you can improve by listening to critics, self-evaluation, and/or emulating your exemplars.

Critics
- Who are the key critics for you to listen to?
- What are their criteria?
- When you read/listen to their criticism, what new option-spring to mind?

Self-evaluation

- How do you know when you have fallen short of your own standards?
- What is most likely to cause this?
- How can you avoid it?

Exemplars

- Who are your exemplars? In your own field? In other fields?
- What qualities do you admire in them?
- How can you use their example to spur you on to achieve more?

NOTE

Seamus Heaney, "Yeats as an Example?" in *Preoccupations: Selected Prose 1968–1978* (Faber and Faber, 1980)

202

CHAPTER 35

Your heart, your ego, and your reputation

We often hear that we shouldn't take misguided or malicious criticism seriously. We should 'let it go' or 'rise above it.'

But what if it's having a negative effect on your public image? What if an untrue allegation or rumor is affecting your career or business? Shouldn't you do something about it?

And if you do answer back to the critics, how do you do this without looking petty or getting sucked into a nasty argument?

In short: how do you decide whether to respond to negative criticism—and how to do it?

Let's start by asking exactly *who* is being criticized. This may seem obvious, but you are a more complex creature than meets the eye. I invite you to consider three different aspects of yourself: your **heart**, your **ego**, and your **reputation**.

YOUR HEART

You know the truth about yourself in your heart. No one can change this, and ultimately it's what you have to live with.

It's possible to fool the whole world by projecting a false image of yourself. But if you lie or cheat or otherwise let yourself down, the knowledge is there in your heart, eating away at you. Conversely, whatever lies other people may tell about you, they can never touch your heart. Even if your reputation is damaged, however painful that may be, you will know in your heart that the lies are not true, and you have nothing with which to reproach yourself.

Being true to yourself is essential if you want to be happy, but it isn't always sufficient. Very few of us have the equanimity of the Zen master who was falsely accused of fathering the illegitimate child of a teenage girl. When she accused him, and the angry villagers brought him the baby, all he did was exclaim, "Ah so?" He then took the child into his care. With his reputation in tatters, he quietly got on with raising the child for several years. Eventually the truth came out and the real father owned up. The villagers went back to the master, apologized for doubting him, and took the child back to his parents. "Ah so?" said the old man, and quietly resumed teaching Zen.

N.B. Looking into your heart is **not** the same as listening to your Inner Critic! The Inner Critic lives in your head, and gives you the worst possible interpretation of your actions. What you know in your heart is the simple truth, without judgment. The more you practice mindfulness, the easier you will find it to tell the difference between your heart and your Inner Critic.

YOUR EGO

Your ego is your self-image. Or rather your self-important-image! It's how you like to see yourself and how you would like the world to see you. It is fragile—easily broken or bruised. And it's high-maintenance—to preserve your ego, you need to spend a lot of time thinking about yourself and worrying about what other people think of you.

Every time you are pained by incompetent, invalid, or malicious criticism, it's your ego that feels the sting. Deep in your heart, you know the criticism is not justified, so there's no need to get agitated. But your ego goes into overdrive because it feels threatened anytime anyone says anything remotely negative about it.

If you want to succeed, you can't afford to cling onto your ego. Part of the price of success is that some people WILL misunderstand you or fail to give you the benefit of the doubt. And some people will tell lies about you, or criticize you unjustly. And some other people will listen to them and form a negative image of you. They will see you as selfish, greedy, lazy, an egomaniac, or whatever. And whatever you do or say, some people will *never* be persuaded to let go of their negative image of you.

(Remember this next time you hear a juicy piece of gossip and feel tempted to pass it on.)

You have to make your peace with this. You will never persuade everyone that you're wonderful. Trying to do this is a distraction from your real work, and will only make you miserable. Even if you succeeded, you would only be pumping up your ego to monstrous proportions. The most important thing is that you can live with what *you* know about yourself in your heart.

Distinguishing between your heart and your ego is another compelling reason to keep up your mindfulness practice. Learn to recognize the tell-tale signs that your ego is on the prowl!

YOUR REPUTATION

Your reputation is how the people who matter see you. In business, these people are your customers, partners, employees, and suppliers. In your career they are your colleagues, your boss, and your clients or customers. In sport they are your teammates, your coach, and your supporters. In the arts they are your peers, some critics, and your audience.

If you want to sleep well at night, there should be no conflict between your heart and your reputation. It's possible to have a false reputation, so that people think you are much better than you are, but you have to live with yourself, and living a lie is no fun.

Plus you are always liable to be found out... so resist the temptation to cut corners or be economical with the truth when you are building your reputation.

Your reputation is very different to your ego. Your ego is *your own* image of yourself, in your imagination; your reputation is *other people's* image of you, in reality. A bruised ego is not the end of the world, but you should take a threat to your reputation very seriously.

To achieve success, you need to manage your reputation. Not because it makes you feel good, or confirms your sense of self-importance—but because **without a good reputation, you can't get anything important done**. Unless the people who matter respect and trust you, you can't do your work, move your projects forward and achieve your mission.

So if criticism threatens to damage your reputation, it's up to you to set the record straight. Sometimes you can do this with words. And it's essential that you do it with actions —staying true to your principles and doing things that make it abundantly clear that the criticism has no foundation.

Here are some options for protecting your reputation, in ascending order of seriousness.

- **ALERT YOUR ALLIES**—don't do or say anything publicly, but make sure your allies (valued, trusted, and influential people in your network) know the truth. This may be all that is needed. And sometimes your allies will come up with helpful suggestions.

- **MAKE A PUBLIC STATEMENT**—publish it on your website, read it to the press, or present it in some other public forum. And only do this after you have run it by your trusted advisers.
- **GET LEGAL ADVICE**—if you think someone has overstepped the mark from rudeness to defamation, consult a legal adviser about your options. Suing them is the most drastic, but there may well be others at your disposal— such as getting their ISP to take down offending content from their website. And be very careful about anything you publish online, even a tweet or Facebook update—in most countries, this counts as publication for legal purposes, so anything you say could have legal implications.

Whatever you do, don't confuse your reputation with your ego. This is extremely difficult, especially when it comes to an emotive issue like criticism. Your ego is very good at persuading you that you need to take it as seriously as your reputation! If in doubt, ask your best friend or mentor—they should be able to help you distinguish between the two.

YOUR NEXT STEPS

Next time you are faced with hostile criticism or a malicious accusation:

1. LOOK IN YOUR HEART
Is the criticism true? If so, you need to do something about it. If not, you only need to act if it's affecting your reputation.

Watch out for the Inner Critic! Don't confuse it with your heart—a friend and/or your mindfulness practice will help you distinguish between the two.

2. WHAT DOES YOUR EGO MAKE OF IT?

Sure signs that your ego is getting involved:

- You keep replaying the criticism/accusation in your mind.
- You worry obsessively about what others will think of you.
- Your mind is filled with thoughts of revenge.
- You feel sorry for yourself and tell yourself you don't deserve it, in a 'poor me' tone of voice.

Don't beat yourself up if you have not yet transcended your ego (I know I haven't). If you catch yourself doing any of these things, snap into mindfulness in order to lessen the ego's hold on you.

3. DOES IT AFFECT YOUR REPUTATION?

- Who is likely to hear and believe the criticism/accusation?
- How important is their opinion to your reputation?
- Who *needs* to know that it's not true?
- What can you say or publish to set the record straight?
- What can you do to demonstrate your integrity?
- Remember, if it's a serious accusation, get advice before saying or publishing anything in public.

NOTE

Paul Reps, *Zen Flesh, Zen Bones*, (Arkana / Penguin, 1991)

CHAPTER 36

When it gets personal

This shouldn't happen but of course it does. Instead of critiquing your work, somebody makes it personal by attacking your personality, appearance, weight, skin color, background, or something else that is irrelevant but hurtful.

Personal abuse is bad enough in private, and can feel a lot worse when it's done in a public forum, especially if others join in. You wouldn't be human if it didn't hurt.

AT HOME

If you're lucky, your home is a refuge, full of loving, supportive, and encouraging people who are right behind you in the pursuit of your dreams. Sadly this isn't true for everyone.

There are few things more challenging than having your confidence undermined by people close to you, who know you well enough to home in on your most sensitive spots. Sometimes this is done out of ignorance or a misguided desire to help—they think they know what's best for you, even when they patently don't. This can be annoying but bearable as long as you have a basically strong relationship. Much harder is when the personal comments stem from malice or jealousy.

Your basic options are:

- **PUT UP WITH IT**—if it's not too serious, not malicious, and temporary.
- **ASSERT YOURSELF**—make it clear that you won't tolerate personal insults. Challenge them every time they insult you.
- **GET HELP**—find an ally (inside the family or out) who can help you challenge the insults, or at least rebuild your confidence.
- **LEAVE**—a last resort, and easier for some than others. If you have a choice and the situation is intolerable, ask yourself whether you really need to tolerate it.

IN YOUR SOCIAL CIRCLE

Notice I didn't say 'among friends.' We've all said nasty things we regret in the heat of an argument, but no true friend will subject you to ongoing personal abuse.

Here you have similar options to a family situation, except that the ties that bind you to the group are weaker. Unlike family, friendship is a matter of choice. And the balance of power relationships is not normally so uneven. So you can be bolder about asserting yourself and quicker to end the relationship if the other person continues the abuse. Why try to be friends with someone who does that?

Don't confuse the desire to belong with friendship. The power of the group can be very intimidating, and there may be situations where you go along with its wishes for the sake of a quiet (or safe) life. But you know in your heart who your friends are.

AT WORK

Abuse in the workplace is very like abuse within a family in one respect—there are reasons to be with these people whether or not you like them. You can feel trapped, and unable to escape or even report the abuse.

Depending on where you live, the laws against workplace abuse may be strong or weak. But even if the law gives you a lot of protection in theory, in practice it takes a lot of courage, stress, and effort to mount a legal challenge against an employer. And some individuals are very devious in the way they target people while staying within the letter of the law.

As with the family, your options depend on your own role and the power relationships within the group. If the insults are coming from your boss it's a lot harder to challenge than if they come from one of your peers.

Again, you can choose to put up with it, assert yourself, get help, or leave. One question it's worth considering is: **Can you really see yourself doing your best work in this environment?** If not, you might be better off leaving regardless of whether or not you have a 'good case' and could succeed in a challenge.

ONLINE TROLLS

We've already met the trolls. The bad news is that the spread of digital communications means the trolls are multiplying and becoming more of a problem. The good news is that police and authorities in many countries are actively finding and punishing the sad characters who do this. Trolls are finding to their cost that although they think they can hide behind a fake name, this is often an illusion.

Because of the virtual nature of their habitat, the usual options don't always work with trolls. Asserting yourself can play into their hands, since they love the attention. And these days it's hard to leave the internet. Some of them will go away if you ignore them.

But if they don't, it is often possible to track down a troll and get the authorities to hold them to account.

Technical and legal changes mean your best options for dealing with trolls are liable to change, but as well as reporting them to the police, you may want to consider reporting them to online service providers whose technology they use, such as Twitter, Facebook, their web host, or email providers.

YOUR NEXT STEPS

When faced with personal abuse, in addition to the options outlined above, consider the effect on your heart, ego, and reputation.

1. YOUR HEART

The first place to look is in your heart. Do you have anything to be ashamed of? Or are the insults merely ignorant or malicious? Next, talk to people who know you well and care about you. What do they make of it? Even if they don't have a magic wand, it can make a huge difference to know that the people who matter still think you are great.

2. YOUR EGO

Obviously, your ego won't like the abuse. And who can blame it? That said, there are two things you need to focus on here:

- **Don't let the abuse ruin your mood.** You probably won't feel great, but don't let the ego's ranting and agonizing overwhelm your day. Again, your mindfulness practice will be critical here.
- **Don't let the ego prompt you to do something you will later regret** e.g. lashing out (verbally or physically), trading insults, or doing anything that could put you in the wrong.

3. YOUR REPUTATION

It's critical—and very difficult—to distinguish between your ego and your reputation, because your ego will be telling you that all kinds of dodgy things are a reasonable and justifiable response, in order to protect your reputation.

Sometimes the person dishing out the abuse will be so obviously laughable and lacking in influence that there's no danger of damage to your reputation. But if you think their words could harm your reputation, look at Chapter 35 for suggestions on protecting it.

4. IF YOU EVER THINK YOU MAY BE IN PHYSICAL DANGER

Make sure other people know about your concerns—including at least one person who can be trusted to raise the alarm if you go missing.

Contact the police or other relevant authorities. No, they don't always respond the way they should, but if the situation is as serious as you fear, you need to alert them.

CHAPTER 37

How to deal with incompetent criticism

So you've worked really hard, burning the midnight oil, to produce
your very best work and present it to someone who matters—a
client, boss, teacher, interviewer, or other such gatekeeper.

You're proud of your work and excited to see what they make
of it. You're convinced they will love it as much as you do. You
can't wait to see their faces, and hear what they have to say. You
hold your breath and smile.

And the response goes something like this:

"Oh dear."
"No good."
"Can't you do better than that?"
"Utterly useless."
"This is a disaster."
"I can't believe you spent all that time to produce this junk."
"Did you *read* the brief?"
"Total crap!"
"Why should I pay for that?"
"I hate it."

And this is someone whose opinion counts. You can't ignore
them. You are expected to respond.

WHAT DO YOU DO?

Firstly, recognize that you are in the presence of an **incompetent critic**.

No matter how bad or unsuitable your work may be, there are ways of critiquing it constructively and respectfully, and this kind of response is neither. Whether they are doing it out of ignorance, tactlessness, or pure spite, this is substandard criticism.

Secondly, ask yourself whether you *really* need to engage with them. If this is an audition or interview, maybe not. If it's a meeting with your boss or an important client, you have less room to maneuver.

Don't get defensive I know this is easier said than done when someone attacks you, but it will inevitably lead to an argument. And whoever wins the argument, you lose: if they win, you have to accept the incompetent criticism; if you win, they probably won't forgive you, and will do what they can to make life difficult.

Don't get aggressive Again, easier said than done. But again, it will only lead to an argument, which doesn't help you.

So how do you respond to an attack without being offensive or aggressive?

When faced with a physical attack, an aikido practitioner aims to blend with the energy of the attacker and either neutralize or redirect it, so that neither you nor the attacker are injured. So a punch doesn't lead to injury or more punches—it leads to an armlock or a swift pivot that leaves the attacker facing the opposite direction, with his intended victim behind him.

When it comes to aggressive feedback, I suggest you practice 'verbal aikido.' Here's how:

1. Clarify the criticism.
2. Ask solution-focused questions.

1. CLARIFY THE CRITICISM

Although your instinct may be to either justify yourself (defensive) or argue back (aggressive), resist the temptation.

Instead, **ask questions** to clarify exactly what the critic means, and **listen carefully** to the answers.

For example:

> "OK this is important. I want to understand exactly what you are concerned about. Are you saying...?"

By saying "this is important" you signal that you are paying attention and taking account of their point of view—but without agreeing or disagreeing. And by saying you want to understand them, and summarizing their words, you are demonstrating your willingness to listen.

If you do this well, it should have the effect of taking the wind out of the critic's sails—after all, it's hard to resist somebody who is doing their best to understand you! Remember, clarifying the criticism does *not* mean you accept it. All you are doing is making sure both of you understand exactly what the critic is unhappy about.

Remember the characteristics of destructive criticism from Chapter 24?

- Lack of perspective
- Vague
- No examples
- Irrelevant
- Exaggerated
- Disrespectful

I'll take each of these in turn, and suggest ways of clarifying them.

LACK OF PERSPECTIVE
The critic speaks as though he or she is the ultimate authority, and does not have the self-awareness to realize that he or she is a human being with a limited viewpoint.

What to do about it
Remind the critic that they may have a valid point of view, but it has limitations:

> "I can understand how it looks to you from your perspective, and I'd like to check whether…"

Another option is to rephrase the criticism in a way that makes it clear the critic is speaking from a particular viewpoint:

> "So from a marketing viewpoint you're saying… ?"

Note that this simultaneously validates the speaker's perspective, and subtly underlines the fact that it is an individual viewpoint and therefore limited.

VAGUE
The critic dismisses the work in general terms, without making the criteria for judgment clear. Typical terms used include 'no good,' 'terrible,' 'not up to scratch,' and 'not fit for purpose.' And of course there's the classic, "I'll know it when I see it."

What to do about it
Ask the critic to spell out their criteria.

> "What criteria are you basing your judgment on?"

> "When you say it doesn't look right, do you mean the structure and layout, or the colors and fonts?"

"Which specific aspect didn't you like?"

NO EXAMPLES

The critic fails to back up their judgment with specific examples as evidence.

What to do about it

Ask for concrete examples and evidence.

"Can you give me a specific example of what you mean?"

"When you say performance hasn't been good enough, what evidence are you basing that on?"

IRRELEVANT

The critic introduces irrelevant criteria, or focuses on an irrelevant aspect of the work.

For example, the client who hates an advert based on her own taste, without considering that her customers' taste may be different. Or the boss who criticizes the color scheme of a website prototype, forgetting that he is supposed to be assessing the layout. Or the marketer who is obsessed with generating lots of web traffic, oblivious of the fact that the company only needs to attract a small number of high-value clients.

What to do about it

Highlight the hidden assumption in the critic's words, and explain why it is not valid. It helps if you can present hard evidence such as robust data.

"I understand that the ad sets your teeth on edge, and we have a lot of evidence that your customers love it."

"You're probably right about the colors, and at this stage we are only concerned with the layout. What do you think of that?"

"It sounds like you're assuming we need to generate a lot of traffic for this website to succeed, but that isn't necessarily the case. Instead of attracting lots of people, we only need to attract a few of the *right* people."

EXAGGERATED

Sweeping, black-and-white judgments, with no acknowledgment of fine grades of quality, or alternative points of view.

Typical words that crop up here include 'terrible,' 'awful,' 'useless,' 'shit,' 'total,' 'utter,' and 'disaster.'

What to do about it

As with vague criticism, ask for specifics:

"Can you be more specific please?"

"You say it's terrible. There are a lot of ways something can be terrible. What exactly do you mean?"

Another approach is to use contrast to demonstrate the absurdity of the critic's position:

"You say you can't possibly sign off a budget of $100,000 at the drop of a hat, but nobody is asking you to do that. We discussed running a pilot for a cost of $10,000—all I'm asking for is permission to proceed with that."

"You say it's a total disaster. To me, a total disaster would mean nobody was buying it. What we are seeing is average sales, which isn't ideal, but it's not a disaster."

"You say it's useless. In fact the performance tests are showing it's above average in three out of the five key areas. What we need to do is find a way to fix the other two."

Beware of sounding too confrontational with this approach! Your tone of voice is critical, as is sticking to concrete facts.

DISRESPECTFUL
The critic is rude, aggressive, or otherwise insensitive to your feelings.

What to do about it
This is the one area where I recommend you stand your ground from the start, and make it clear that the critic's comments are unacceptable. Call them out and make it clear that you don't accept rudeness or personal abuse.

> "We're here to talk about the work, so please don't make personal comments."

> "If you're not happy with my work, that's one thing. But I don't need to take insults like that."

In some industries, sadly, insults and bad behavior are rife, and considered just part of the culture. If you want to get on, you have to put up with it. If you're working in a place like that, you may decide the benefits are worth it. Personally I can't imagine doing my best work with people who don't show me basic respect, so I'd look for an alternative. But it's your call.

2. ASK SOLUTION-FOCUSED QUESTIONS

By asking questions, listening and summarizing, you are *not* accepting the critic's point of view, merely trying to understand it. If you can repeat their critique back to them, and get them to give you a word or nod of agreement, you have taken the first step towards a more productive relationship.

The next step is to start asking **solution-focused questions**, to get the critic to buy into a *potential* solution to the problem they have identified. As the name suggests, a solution-focused question is one that switches the focus of attention from problems (where it's easy to get bogged down in arguments) to solutions. When you agree on a mutually desirable outcome, it becomes a lot easier to move things forward.

The moment when you move from problem-talk to solution-talk is like the moment when the aikido practitioner, having firmly grasped the attacker's arm, pivots to redirect the momentum in a new direction.

Here are some typical solution-focused questions:

"What would your ideal solution look like?"

"If I delivered the best possible performance for you, what would you see me doing that I haven't done up to now?"

"What has to be included in the final version for you to sign this off?"

When facing criticism, you can switch the conversation from problems to solutions by following up your summary of the criticism with a solution-focused question.

For example:

"OK the ad isn't to your taste, but if I could show you evidence that it's boosting sales, would you be willing to roll it out?"

"So you're concerned that the website won't attract a lot of traffic. But if I can demonstrate an improved conversion rate, bringing you more customers, would you be happy to proceed?"

"So there were some things you liked about my presentation, but you felt my slides and handouts weren't up to standard. If I can fix those elements, will you give me another chance?"

"It sounds like you're assuming X—but if I can show you that X is not necessary, would you be willing to consider an alternative?"

These questions paint a picture of a positive outcome and invite the critic to buy into it, at least as a possibility.

If she doesn't, and if you can't get her to describe *any* future scenario that would satisfy her, then you've reached the end of the line. You are not going to be able to please this person, so it's better if you accept that now, and end the working relationship. At the very least, you will look positive and professional. You also have the satisfaction of knowing you didn't just come out with a knee-jerk response—you gave it your best shot, gave them the chance to have a different kind of conversation, and there wasn't much else you could do.

But if the critic does agree that your proposed solution would be acceptable, and they give you a chance to fix the problem, then something magical has happened. Instead of attacking you, *they are now agreeing with you*. Even if they are not particularly friendly, they start showing you more respect. And you now have a shot at getting the outcome you want.

SUCCESS

226

CHAPTER 38

What does success look like to you?

Let's play a little game…

In a moment, close your eyes and say the word 'success' to yourself.

Then notice what thoughts the word brings to mind, and what feelings it evokes.

Then open your eyes and read the rest of this chapter.

———

How was that?

Were your thoughts positive and encouraging? Were the images on your inner screen full of light and smiles? Did you feel excited and motivated?

Or were your thoughts skeptical and warning? Did you picture successful people as selfish and greedy, the kind of people you wouldn't want to become? Did you feel repulsed by the idea of success?

Did you see success as realistic and attainable for you? Was it like a prize that was within your reach—if only you stretched yourself far enough?

Or did success look hopelessly beyond your grasp? Did you picture the Realm of the Successful like the summit of Mount Olympus in Greek mythology—a place bathed in soothing light, where the elite gather in their spotless robes and sip sparkling liquids, out of bounds to mere mortals like you?

Did you imagine success in terms of its external trappings—money, big houses, flash cars, exotic holidays, a comfortable life for your family, awards ceremonies, and your name in lights?

Or did you think about success in terms of the work you would be doing, and whether you would find it fulfilling and meaningful?

Did you see success in terms of accomplishment—solving an important problem, creating groundbreaking works of art, breaking sporting records, or setting new standards in your field?

Or did you think of it in terms of making a difference to others—helping or inspiring them, and helping to build a better society?

Were your thoughts and feelings about success simple and clear—or were they a mixture of some (or all) of the above? Did you feel confused or conflicted?

A LITTLE GAME WITH BIG IMPLICATIONS

When you play this game, the thoughts that come most easily to mind are a good indicator of your image of success. And how you *see* success—even subconsciously—influences how you *feel* about success. And how you feel about it influences how you *act* towards it.

If success looks attractive, attainable, and acceptable to you, you will instinctively move towards it. Even when things get tough, you will find yourself digging deep and unearthing solutions when you need them.

If success looks repulsive, dangerous, or immoral to you, you'll instinctively move away from it. Even when you're consciously striving to succeed, you'll find yourself sabotaging your best efforts by making 'stupid' mistakes.

If success looks unattainable, you'll find it hard to stay motivated. Whenever you encounter the slightest difficulty, a part of you will sigh 'What's the point?' and look for any excuse to give up and save yourself the pain of disappointment.

And if success is a mixture of any (or all) of the above, you will feel pulled in different directions. Your motivation will ebb and flow. You will risk being paralyzed by indecision (a.k.a. procrastination).

TIME TO CHANGE YOUR MIND ABOUT SUCCESS?

This little game has shown you how success looks to you *now*. Your current image of success is partly of your own making and partly inherited from your parents, family, friends, and popular culture.

If you're lucky, you'll have an image of success that you find attractive and motivating—in which case, feel free to move on to the next chapter. But if you have any doubts or hesitations, it's time to change your mind. Time to stop seeing success in the same old way, and start *imagining* it in a new way.

For a long time, I struggled with two conflicting images of success: on the one hand, as a poet, I aspired to artistic success and saw business as evil; while on the other, I hated the idea of getting a 'proper' job, so as a freelancer I wanted a successful business. It was hard for me to focus on writing poetry when I was stressed about money; but when I tried to focus on building up the business, it felt like selling out, so I ended up sabotaging myself. It was a great recipe for misery, and it was my staple diet for years.

Fortunately Shakespeare came to the rescue.

Once I looked beyond the stereotype of the Romantic poet, it struck me as slightly odd that the man who wrote the greatest poetry in English was also a highly successful entrepreneur. As a shareholder in one of London's leading theater companies,

Shakespeare wrote popular entertainment for money, in one of the dodgiest neighborhoods of the city. As well as building his theater business, he was a property speculator and money-lender, earning enough to not only live well in the capital but also buy the biggest house in his home town of Stratford-upon-Avon. And in the midst of all this, he wrote his mind-blowing poetry.

Shakespeare gave me a new image of success, by showing me that it's possible to combine creative and commercial achievement. Whenever I feel the old conflict between the two, I ask myself, "What would Shakespeare do?" I usually get the feeling he would shrug his shoulders and get on with it—whether 'it' was a poetic problem or a business challenge—and wonder what all the fuss was about.

YOUR NEXT STEPS

1.   If you're struggling to think of success in a positive light, take a piece of paper and write all the answers you can think of to the question: 'What's wrong with success?'

2.   Now think of someone you admire who achieved success in the field(s) you are working in.

What makes them a success in your eyes?

How did *they* see success? (If you're not sure, read up on their life and opinions.)

What would they say about your list of things that are wrong with success?

3.   Now take another sheet of paper and use it to construct an image of success that you find truly inspiring and attractive.

First, list all the different categories that are important to you. Then under each heading list out all the things that you want to achieve in that category.

To get you started, here are some category suggestions:

- **PERSONAL FULFILMENT**—the things you want to do for the sheer pleasure and satisfaction they give you.
- **PROFESSIONAL ACHIEVEMENT**—milestones you want to reach, records you want to break, awards you want to win.
- **FINANCIAL TARGETS**— how much you want to earn, and what you want to do with it.
- **LEARNING**—the skills, knowledge, experience, and wisdom you want to acquire.
- **IMPACT**—the difference you want to make to the world and the people in it.

232

CHAPTER 39

How much do you want it?

Admit it: you're ambitious.

You're reading this book because you have big dreams and you want to turn them into reality. You want to succeed.

But it's not really the done thing to say so, is it?

These days, 'ambition' is a dirty word. People who are ambitious are viewed as either selfish or unrealistic. ("That sounds a bit ambitious," is code for, "You are going to fail.") Yet it wasn't always this way.

The poet James Fenton points out that 500 years ago in Renaissance Florence, artists had no qualms about admitting their ambitions. Discussing Giorgio Vasari's biography of Andrea del Verrocchio, he points out that Verrocchio became a sculptor because there was 'much to be gained' in that field i.e. honor. When he felt he had won as much honor as possible as a sculptor, he took up painting, only to realize he could never match Leonardo da Vinci—at which point he gave up and went back to sculpture again.

In Renaissance Florence, there was no shame in seeking glory as an artist—only glory. Even if you failed, it was still regarded as a noble ambition. Naturally, there was an ugly side to this: the competition was fierce and sometimes violent. But I still think we lost something important when we made a tacit agreement to keep quiet about our ambition. (Of course we didn't get rid of it.) Because if you don't acknowledge your ambition—even to yourself—you risk choking it. You risk not only falling short of the best that you could do, but not even attempting it.

And I don't think you have to be a Machiavellian monster to achieve success. If you're ambitious purely for yourself—for your fame, status, riches, and place in history—then clearly ambition is going to corrupt you. But if you're ambitious primarily *for your work*—for how far you can take it, for what you can achieve, for the impact it can have on others— then I believe it's still possible to think in terms of a noble ambition.

I remember the day I realized I was ambitious, right down to the very moment. The train was pulling into the platform, the sun flashed from the windows as they rolled past, and it suddenly struck me that I had big ambitions. I wanted to do things on a larger scale, make more of an impression, more of a difference than I had done before.

And once the cat was out of the bag, my excuses were gone. I was committed—to hard work, to pushing through the wall of fear, to somehow finding a way to make it happen. (This was years before I discovered blogging and the possibility of reaching a global audience from my laptop, so that last part wasn't clear *at all*.) The upside was that once I admitted my ambition, I opened the door to a marvelous adventure—to the fun of experimenting, exploring, and connecting with like-minded people, and to delivering outsize results for the effort I put in.

You don't need to turn into an egomaniac. You don't need to walk over people or stab them in the back. You don't need to spend hours admiring yourself in the mirror and polishing your awards. You don't even need to tell your ambition to another soul. All you need to do is admit it—to yourself—and give yourself permission to pursue it.

And do it soon. It may feel as though we're going to live forever, but for each of us there's a window of opportunity that will close if we wait too long. Don't leave it too late.

YOUR NEXT STEPS

1.   Take a sheet of paper and write down your noble ambitions—for your work, your business, your career, and/or your life.

How does it feel to admit your ambitions?

How does your future look now?

What do you need to start (or keep) doing this week, to keep yourself on track to achieve your noble ambitions?

2.   Now take another sheet of paper and write down your *ignoble* ambitions—what you consider the 'wrong' goals for you to focus on, that could distract you from your noble ambition.

For example, if you're an actor, your noble ambition might be to perfect your art and captivate audiences with your performances. An ignoble ambition might be to rub your rivals' noses in your success.

How does *that* list make you feel?

How can you avoid the temptations of your *ignoble* ambitions?

NOTES

James Fenton, "A Lesson from Michelangelo," *The Strength of Poetry* (Oxford University Press, 2001)

A version of this chapter was first published at 99u.com

CHAPTER 40

Fear of success

Yes, this really does happen.

Quite a few people have consulted me because they were on the verge of a major success, and found themselves sabotaging their chances with 'stupid' mistakes and 'irrational' behavior.

- Saying something daft in a sales meeting.
- Fluffing easy lines in an audition.
- Procrastinating and missing critical deadlines.
- Overlooking important details.

So what's going on here?

Surely we *want* success?

We put enough time and effort into achieving it, we go through enough suffering to reach it, we work hard at developing the resilience that will get us there. What's not to like?

It boils down to fear.

Yes, success is a wonderful thing. But every silver lining has a cloud. The closer you get to achieving your goal, the more the implications of success begin to dawn on you—and some of them can be daunting.

This kind of fear is actually a very positive sign. It shows you're nearing another important threshold—and as always on the Hero's Adventure, a Threshold Guardian rises up to test you. But if you face down the fear and rise to the challenge, the Guardian will give way and allow you to enjoy the rewards.

Let's consider three of the most common fears associated with success.

1. FEAR OF NOT COPING WITH SUCCESS

When clients tell me about this one, I sometimes ask—gently, humorously: "How did you cope with failure? That was no picnic either!"

In most cases, we cope with failure and difficulty one step at a time. Sometimes we feel overwhelmed, but we generally muddle through. There's no reason why success should be any different. If you look at it all at once, it *will* feel overwhelming—so don't look at it all at once! Just focus on the next challenge, the next step.

And the nice thing about success is you typically have more resources to call on than when you were struggling. You have money to solve some problems, and people around you to help with others. Your reputation can open doors. And achieving any measure of success can give a big boost to your confidence—as long as you give yourself credit for your achievement.

2. FEAR OF SELLING OUT

To some people, selling out means earning a lot of money, living in a big house, driving a fast car, or having your picture in all the papers. If that's your definition of selling out, it will obviously reduce your options. And if it also happens to be your definition of success, you have a big problem!

Personally, I don't think selling out means having material possessions or worldly fame. I think it's perfectly possible to have those things without being a sell-out. To me, it comes down to your motivation—selling out means becoming cynical, satisfied to turn out mediocre work in pursuit of this kind of reward. Maybe you and I wouldn't care if we reached the point where it became easy to earn rewards without merit, but I like to think we would.

The most important thing is to stay motivated by the work itself, and the positive difference it can make in the world, rather than any rewards you receive after the fact. If your work is driven by fascination, inspiration, fun, freedom, or a sense of purpose, then in a sense it's irrelevant whether you are a millionaire or muddling along financially, a celebrity or a nobody.

Not everyone will see it that way, of course. And your ego may not like some of the things these people say about you. But the only person who really knows the truth about this is you, and the only place you'll find the answer is your heart.

3. FEAR OF BECOMING SOMEONE ELSE

Because we habitually put successful people on a pedestal, the idea of becoming 'one of them' can feel daunting. You start to worry that you'll turn into someone else, a person your friends and family don't recognize—and don't like.

This fear has some foundation. After all, if you were completely satisfied with who you are now, you wouldn't be on this quest, would you?

One of the main reasons for pursuing an adventure is to fulfill your own potential, discovering and expressing new parts of your personality. And maybe some people won't be comfortable with that, and will say you've changed like it's not a compliment. But who's on your side here? Is this really about you? Do you want to hold yourself back to fit someone else's cardboard cutout image of 'the real you'?

Look at it the other way round. Would you want a friend or family member to sell themselves short for fear of conforming to *your* expectations of them? Or would you feel thrilled for them, and want to encourage them to become all they can be? (And maybe want a little reassurance that they haven't forgotten you, and love you just as much as ever?)

Think of the process of change as *adding* to who you are, not taking away. Yes, your public image and persona may change. You will hopefully discover new and exciting facets of your character. But that doesn't necessarily mean you have to throw away all the old ones.

If you've ever gone back to your home town after some time away, you may have experienced 'social re-entry'—returning to your family and friends, feeling strange and different at first, but then revisiting old haunts, hanging out with old friends, and slipping back into old habits of speech.

No, you'll never be exactly the same person you once were. But that will be true whether you stay still or pursue your dreams. You are more complex and interesting than the cardboard cut-out. Accept and celebrate the fact.

YOUR NEXT STEPS

1. NOT COPING WITH SUCCESS
a) If you feel intimidated or overwhelmed at the thought of all the demands success will bring, start by making a list of them—the small ones as well as the big ones.

b) Now take each one in turn and rate it on a scale of 1–10, where 1 = you are completely incapable of dealing with it, and 10 = supremely confident of coping just fine. Sometimes this is all you need to do—just realizing that one or two big challenges are looming disproportionately large can help you get back your sense of perspective.

c)   Now make a list of all the resources you have—or will have if you succeed—that were unavailable to you in the past.
   For example:

- Knowledge
- Skills
- Experience
- Money
- Time
- Assistance
- Mentors and teachers
- A network of influential people
- A reputation that opens doors

d)   Now join the dots between the challenges and your resources. Next to each challenge, write down the resources that will help you tackle it. Again, this may be all you need to do—if you realize you already have, or will shortly have, all the resources you need to rise to the challenge.

e)   Finally check to see if you are missing any resources that are essential for overcoming an important challenge. If so, set yourself a goal of acquiring the necessary resources. For example, if you're daunted by the thought of doing media interviews, look for some specialist training. Or if you don't think you'll be able to keep up with the admin, look into hiring a part-time or virtual assistant.

2.   SELLING OUT

I've given you my definition of selling out, but for this to be meaningful, you need to be clear about your own definition. Start by asking:

- What does selling out mean to you?
- What's the line you don't want to cross?
- How will you know if you're in danger of crossing it?

Next, think of the people who might accuse you of selling out.

- What does selling out mean to *them*?
- What's the line they don't want you to cross?
- Does it really matter to *you* if you cross it?

3.   FEAR OF BECOMING SOMEONE ELSE

a)   Close your eyes and imagine you can see yourself in the future—the 'successful you' who has achieved your goals and made your dreams come true.

What do you like about the person you see?

Are there any things you *dislike* about that person, or things that make you feel uncomfortable? If so, make a list of them.

b)   Now go through the list and ask yourself:

How likely is it that I will really become like this?

If the answer is 'not very,' you can safely cross that item off the list.

c) Now look at the remaining items on the list—these are the things that make you feel uncomfortable, and that you think are fairly or highly likely to come true. For each of these, ask yourself:

Am I uncomfortable because this goes against my personal values—or because of the expectations of other people?

If the former, you need to take steps to make sure this doesn't happen. Success at the price of your integrity is not worth it.

If the latter, you'll need to steel yourself to accept potential rejection and criticism from these people. (And maybe revisit the earlier chapters of this book...)

244

SUCCESS

CHAPTER 41

No, you don't need confidence

When I was 24 and floundering around for a direction in life, my therapist said to me: "You know, you could do *this* if you want to." I was dumbstruck.

"But don't you have to be old and wise to be a therapist?"

Apparently not.

Inspired by her enthusiasm, I started reading books about hypnotherapy, neuro-linguistic programming, psychology, meditation, yoga. I went to my local library and asked what books they had about hypnosis. The librarian looked stern and told me I'd have to make an appointment with the Head Librarian. When I was eventually ushered into his office, he asked me why I wanted to see the hypnosis books and what I was going to do with them.

"We're very careful with these books now. Last year someone started reading one of them in the library and went into a trance, and we couldn't get him out again. Ever since then, we keep them locked away in the stack."

Books so dangerous they need to be kept under lock and key? *Let me at them!*

I researched hypnotherapy colleges, sent out applications, and was thrilled to be accepted on my chosen course. It felt like I'd been let in by mistake. I saw trainers demonstrate jaw-dropping hypnotic feats—arm levitation, catalepsy, amnesia, analgesia, time distortion, age regression. Would I ever be able to do such things myself?

During my therapy training I spent time as a freelance copy editor. One day during coffee break at a publisher's office, I let slip that I was studying hypnosis. One of my co-workers stared at me in astonishment. She couldn't help blurting out:

"But don't you have to be charismatic to do that?"

Evidently not.

In the end, I not only qualified as a therapist, I also went on to teach on the same hypnotherapy course—and demonstrate the various amazing hypnotic feats to open-mouthed students.

A few years later, I was a partner in a small business coaching consultancy, providing executive coaching and training to large corporations. Out of the blue, one of the two senior partners suggested I take over new business development, a.k.a. Sales. "I think you'd be good at it," he said.

Once more, I was flabbergasted.

"But don't you have to be an extrovert to do that?"

Maybe not.

That was the start of my adventures in sales, which (as we saw in Chapter 21) turned out to be surprisingly successful, in spite of my lack of knowledge, experience, or an extrovert personality.

Over and over, I've heard from clients:

"I can't do that because I don't have enough X."

For 'X', read 'confidence', 'talent', 'experience', 'motivation', 'self-esteem', or some other mysterious quality that we imagine we need to have *before* we attempt to achieve our goals.

But the thing is, you don't need to be old, wise, confident, charismatic, outgoing, talented, experienced, or anything else before you *set out* on the road to success. All you need to do is focus on your goal, get started, and keep your eyes and ears open along the way.

As time goes on you will make plenty of mistakes and improve by learning from them. You will have little triumphs that boost your confidence. And gradually, you will probably start to *look* confident, charismatic, outgoing, talented, or whatever. And maybe people will start sticking those labels on you, as if you were lucky enough to be born with all the qualities required for success.

But you'll know different.

Confidence is like physique—while some of us are naturally more muscular than others, we can all develop what we have if we're prepared to put in the hard work and embrace the pain. Waiting for 'confidence' before pursuing success is as absurd as waiting for your muscles to grow before you pick up a dumbbell.

YOUR NEXT STEPS

1. If you don't feel you have what it takes to succeed, take a sheet of paper and make a list of all the qualities you wish you had more of, but are sadly lacking—such as confidence, charisma, wisdom, or experience.

2. Now take a second sheet and list all the things you could and would do if only you had the qualities on your first list.

3. Pick one of the items on your second list and do it anyway.

No, you don't have the magical qualities required, so that means there's no pressure on you to actually succeed—just have a go and see what happens.

4. Keep working your way through your 'action list', and see what you learn from it. (Beware: small signs of success may lead to symptoms of the onset of confidence.)

CHAPTER 42

Building momentum

At the start of 2006 I took a leap of faith by adding a blog to my website at www.wishfulthinking.co.uk, and devoting lots of time to writing posts, networking with other bloggers, and learning everything I could about blogging and online marketing.

The idea was to market my coaching business, but back then, particularly in the UK, blogging was very new, and it was anything but a proven marketing strategy. So I had plenty of well-meaning friends and colleagues warning me of the dangers of giving away too much valuable advice for free. Another common response I got was this one:

"I don't know how you find the time."

Now superficially, this looks like a compliment, but often the implication was pretty clear: if you've got time to burn on blogging, you can't be doing anything important.

The answer is that I found the time by getting up early to write the blog, and 'forgetting' to buy a TV when I moved to a new flat. I ploughed away at the blog month after month, while trying to ignore the nagging voice at the back of my head, asking me whether I was *sure* I really wanted to give away so much advice for free, and shouldn't I be doing something more productive?

It took several months before I started to see tangible results, but when it happened, it was worth it: emails from creative directors and training managers, asking whether I could provide coaching or training for their teams. The kind of people who would not have taken my phone call a few months earlier. The kind of clients I dreamed of landing, and they were contacting *me*. I had gone through the wall of fear, and out the other side.

In 2006 I published 70 blog posts and attracted a total of 12,000 unique visitors to my website. By 2011 I was doing most of my blogging at lateralaction.com, so I published just six posts at wishfulthinking.co.uk—but the site still attracted 200,000 unique visitors, and plenty of new business, with minimal maintenance.

So how come my Wishful Thinking blog now enables me to achieve bigger results with less effort than before?

Momentum.

Over the years, the site has attracted several thousand subscribers, as well as links from other websites. The links have boosted my search engine rankings, so Google sends me plenty of visitors. I've published a string of free ebooks that have been downloaded hundreds of thousands of times, all containing links back to my homepage. And the posts I publish are not only sent out to the subscribers, but are also promoted to several thousand more people via my accounts on Twitter, Facebook and Google+. Last but not least, all of the above mean that on any given week, there are plenty of people sharing my blog posts and ebooks, forwarding emails to their contacts, and helping to spread the word about who I am and what I do.

Whatever you set out to do, you'll probably find a similar pattern.

To begin with, it feels scary and uncertain. Maybe you don't know anyone who has done this before. No one around you 'gets' what you are trying to do, and may even try to discourage you. It's a process of trial and error for months or years on end, before you see the light at the end of the tunnel and have something concrete to show for your efforts. But eventually, your momentum builds to the point where it looks unstoppable and inevitable.

There are no guarantees, of course, and in the early days your success will feel anything but unstoppable and inevitable. But you *can* start to detect momentum early, if you know where to look...

Back in 2006, when I was still getting less than 100 monthly visitors to my website, I read an encouraging post by Darren Rowse of ProBlogger.net. At the time, Darren was one of the few people offering high quality, detailed information on how to succeed as a professional blogger. He had something like 12,000 subscribers at that point, which seemed a dizzyingly large number. In this piece, Darren advised new bloggers to stop comparing their subscriber count to established bloggers, since this could easily be discouraging. Instead, he suggested we compare *this* month's stats with those from *last* month. Do you have more subscribers than last month? If so, you're moving in the right direction. You could even plot the figures on a chart, and extrapolate the trend a year or two into the future, and see yourself with hundreds or even thousands of readers. It seemed exciting but improbable at the time, but that's exactly what happened in my case.

So when you're in the early stages, try to blot out the discouraging voices (internal and external) and resist the temptation to compare yourself to people several years down the road. Instead, do your best to build and detect your momentum, by picking one or two key things to measure, and tracking them regularly. No matter how small the numbers are, focus on whether they are getting bigger or smaller every day/week/month. If so, take heart. Success is never guaranteed, but you are slowly and steadily tipping the odds in your favor.

YOUR NEXT STEPS

1. What stage are you at in your journey?

1. **INERTIA**—just setting out, contending with fear and uncertainty.
2. **TRACTION**—starting to see small, incremental (but inconsistent) progress.
3. **MOMENTUM**—clear and consistent progress toward your goals.
4. **UNSTOPPABLE**—nothing's going to hold you back!

2. If you're at the Inertia or Traction stage, ask yourself what metric you can use to track your progress? Here are some possibilities.

- **ATHLETES AND SPORTS PLAYERS**—distance traveled, time taken, weight lifted, pass completion, points scored.
- Entrepreneurs and marketers—new customers, repeat customers, units sold, profits, turnover, mailing list subscribers, sales conversion rates.
- **WRITERS**—words per day/week/month, pieces completed, pieces published or sold.
- **ARTISTS AND CREATIVES**—hours in the studio, works completed, works published or sold.
- **TEACHERS**—attendance figures, test scores, student satisfaction scores.

Then decide how often you're going to measure—daily, weekly, monthly, or after every event you take part in. Try to make it monthly at the longest, otherwise it's hard to feel a sense of momentum. And record your scores somewhere you can easily review them, such as a chart, spreadsheet, or software app.

Of course these are all 'hard' measures, which are more important in fields such as business or sport, where success is more commonly defined in hard numbers. In other fields, such as the arts, success is based on 'soft' measures—quality not quantity.

There's no point writing thousands of words a day if you never improve.

But whatever path you are on, for the purposes of building momentum, it's worth establishing some kind of hard metric, to give you a sense of measurable progress on those days when it feels as though you're getting nowhere.

254

CHAPTER 43

"You're lucky"

Years ago I read an interview with The Cure. Surveying the re-
stored Tudor mansion (owned by Richard Branson) where the
band had recorded their latest album, the interviewers described
the extravagantly comfortable surroundings and the "atmosphere
of pleasant idleness." Robert Smith agreed it was a fun place to
live and work, but made it clear who had earned the comfort:

> "People might say it's easy for us, easy to sit around here for six
> months, but to get here hasn't been easy."

In a 2010 blog post where he shared his thoughts on the (al-
leged) 'death of publishing,' Chris Guillebeau described an article
in which an author complained that the only people who sold
books anymore were the ones with popular blogs.

> This puzzled me. Where does a popular blog come from—does the
> blog fairy descend from the sky with a passionate group of readers,
> all eager to support a new writer? Or does it maybe have something
> to do with consistent, dedicated work over a long period of time?

One of the weird things about success is that people see what
you have, not what it cost you to get it. They stop saying, "You're
crazy," and start saying, "You're lucky." This can be annoying, but

it shouldn't be too hard to see the funny side. Or to enjoy it as a compliment.

NOTES

"Pictures of Youth" interview with The Cure, *Melody Maker*, 7 March 1992

Blog post by Chris Guillebeau: chrisguillebeau.com/3x5/strategy-tactics-and-the-plan-for-the-next-97-days

CHAPTER 44

How to handle praise

"Never interrupt when someone is giving you a compliment."

This is one of the best pieces of advice I ever received, for two reasons.

Firstly, when somebody gives you a gift, it's rude to refuse it. Notice how *you* feel next time you compliment someone and they dismiss it with a wave of their hand. (Do they think you don't know what you're talking about? Or just flattering them?) So the least you can do is to hear them out and thank them for the gift.

Secondly, standing there and taking the compliment forces you to own up to the fact that you are in fact *delighted* to receive it. How many times have you brushed off a compliment in public, only to replay it and savor it in private? Exactly.

So next time someone offers you a compliment, look them in the eye, listen to what they say, then smile and thank them. You will both feel better. And you'll be pleased to discover that acclimatization works just as well for embarrassment as it does for pain and humiliation—after a while, you get used to it and don't feel it so much.

The same goes for praise of any kind—applause, a good review in a magazine, a public 'thank you' from your boss, an award—accept it graciously and enjoy it for what it's worth. But beware of letting it go to your head. Just as you would with criticism, remind yourself that this is the opinion of one person, based on one set of criteria, at one moment in time. There are always alternatives.

And just as you would with criticism, notice the effect praise has on your heart, your ego, and your reputation.

YOUR HEART

If your heart leaps when you are praised, that's a pretty good sign the praise is merited. So enjoy it. You did something great and it probably cost you a lot, so savor the moment.

YOUR EGO

Of course, your ego is thrilled too. But whereas your heart leaps for joy in the moment, your ego carries the praise round like a souvenir, repeating it over and over, and whispering in your ear, embellishing the praise and predicting a marvelous future for you.

Beware! Your ego does this as a way of inflating itself, but if you spend too long listening to it, you'll lose touch with reality. And risk turning into an egomaniac. You've seen it happen to others; don't let it happen to you.

YOUR REPUTATION

Be realistic about the value of each piece of praise to your reputation. If it's from a family member, friend or mentor, that's a special kind of praise, to be savored in private. If it's from a prominent thought leader in your field, you might consider asking for permission to quote it as a testimonial or reference.

Whatever you do with the praise you receive, don't linger over it too long. Acknowledge it as a nice stopping point, but remind yourself there's still a long way to go, and a lot more to be done.

YOUR NEXT STEPS

1.   When receiving praise or compliments in person, always hear the speaker out, look them in the eye, and thank them. Give them the pleasure of seeing that you appreciate their words. If you feel embarrassed, don't worry. The next time will be a little less excruciating...

2.   Whatever kind of praise you receive, notice how it affects your heart, your ego, and your reputation:

- **YOUR HEART**—if you feel a surge of joy, enjoy it. If you don't feel anything much, maybe you should take the praise with a pinch of salt.
- **YOUR EGO**—notice how eager it is to repeat the praise, and flatter you with visions of a glorious future. Don't try to stop it—it's just your ego, and this is what egos do. But don't pay too much attention.
- **YOUR REPUTATION**—if the praise comes from an influential public figure, consider whether it would be appropriate to ask permission to reproduce it as a testimonial or similar.

3.   Remember Martin O'Neill's 48-hour rule—stop and enjoy the praise, but don't stop for too long! Get back to work sooner rather than later.

CHAPTER 45

Be kind

There's a well-known story about the composer Rossini that exists in different versions. The gist of it is that a young composer visits the maestro and asks for feedback on his two latest compositions. Halfway through the first one, Rossini interrupts:

> "You needn't play any more. I prefer the other one."

It's a good story, but it doesn't reflect very well on Rossini. (Let's give him the benefit of the doubt, and assume it's an urban myth.) This kind of thing makes for entertaining talent shows, but anyone who takes delight in delivering clever putdowns to people in a weaker position needs to take a good look in the mirror.

As an undergraduate I was lucky enough to be on the end of a more considerate variation on the Rossini approach to feedback, when the poet Seamus Heaney made himself available to give one-to-one feedback on students' poems. This was before he won the Nobel Prize, but he was still a superstar, whose poetry I had been reading and studying for years. So it's an understatement to say I was nervous as I sat waiting in the corridor with my manuscripts. When it was my turn, he ushered me in and patiently read through the three poems I had brought.

My heart was in my mouth. It was so quiet I could hear him breathe.

Then he looked up with a smile on his face and picked up the first poem. "If I were you," he said, "I would have shown me this one first too." He then went on to talk about what he liked about it, enthusing about the promising bits and encouraging me as much as he could. It was only gradually that it dawned on me that the other two poems probably had none of the redeeming features of the first one. But by that time I didn't really mind, I was so pleased that he had found something he liked and was showing me how to improve it. When he finished by inviting me to submit the poem to a student anthology he was editing, I left the room floating on air.

When it's your turn to critique someone's work, be honest, but not brutally honest. Better to be remembered for your kindness by one 'nobody' than to go down in history as the master of the clever putdown.

CHAPTER 46

Happily ever after?

In 1966 it looked like Brian Wilson had it made.

As the leader and creative genius behind the Beach Boys, he had followed up the critical and commercial success of the album *Pet Sounds* with the smash-hit 'Good Vibrations'—the group's third US No.1 which sold over a million copies. The *Guardian* dubbed him: "America's equivalent of The Beatles with his ability to expand popular taste."

The 'Good Vibrations' sessions ran to many hours, several studios, and a bill for $50,000 due to Wilson's pursuit of perfection. Its success meant his record company forgave him and agreed to bankroll his next project, the ambitious *SMiLE* album. Which is when it all really began to fall apart.

The recording was disrupted by band tensions and litigation and eventually abandoned when Wilson suffered a nervous breakdown. One story described Wilson as 'heartbroken' when he heard excerpts from The Beatles' forthcoming *Sergeant Pepper* album, and felt he could never surpass it with *SMiLE*.

Wilson spent years in the wilderness, suffering from drug addiction and mental health problems. *SMiLE* was spoken of as a legendary 'lost' album and its creator was routinely written off as a tortured genius who had lost his way.

In 2004 he stunned the world by not only completing and releasing *SMiLE*, but performing it in a series of stunning concerts, with a debut performance at the Royal Albert Hall. One of the album tracks won a Grammy for Best Rock Instrumental.

No wonder a Hollywood movie based on Wilson's life is in the pipeline. He is an extreme case, but we can recognize his story as an archetype.

The rock star—like Elvis or Johnny Cash—who finds fame and fortune early on, only to slide into addiction, despair and/or obscurity, before making a rousing comeback late in life.

The entrepreneur—like Walt Disney or Steve Jobs—who achieves wealth and success early on, before losing his Midas touch, going bankrupt or getting fired—but rises again and delivers his biggest triumphs.

The sports legend—like Pélé or Andre Agassi—whose early successes are interrupted by injury and/or personal problems, who is written off before bouncing back to lift more trophies and cement his legendary status.

Even Buddhas may not be immune. Many stories about spiritual quests end with the words "and then he achieved enlightenment," as if this were some final state that resolved all struggle.

Yet in his moving book *After the Ecstasy, the Laundry*, Jack Kornfield relays his conversations with many Tibetan Lamas, Zen masters and other spiritual gurus, who found that even spectacular enlightenment experiences (in monasteries, ashrams, and mountaintop retreats) were followed by all kinds of problems when they returned to the 'real world'—depression, divorce, alcoholism, and lawsuits. True equanimity required them to accept their imperfections, and pick up their teaching from a more humble position.

We often think of 'success' as the end of the story—happily ever after. But more often than not, it's happily in the middle—before another challenge comes along, and another round of striving and failing, rejection and criticism. The cycle ends with another and bigger 'success'—which is wonderful but only a stopping point before the next cycle...

After you've been round the wheel a few times, you have a choice to make—either you get frustrated and disappointed by never reaching your 'journey's end' or you start to enjoy the journey itself, relishing the challenges as well as the rewards, the downs as well as the ups.

YOUR NEXT STEPS

1. Think of a big challenge that you succeeded at.
   When was the point that struggle gave way to success?
   How did you keep yourself going until you reached that point?

2. Now think of a big disappointment you suffered, but recovered from.
   What was the point at which things started to get better?
   How did you pick yourself up?

3. Now think of a time you were hurt by criticism but lived to tell the tale.
   At what point did you start to feel better?
   How did you negate the effect of the criticism?

4. Now think of a big success from your past.
   When did things start to get difficult again?
   Did you resist the new challenge or embrace it?

5. Look back at the big picture of your journey so far, the ups as well as the downs.
   What patterns can you see?

6. Now consider the future.
   How can you remind yourself not to get discouraged when a new challenge appears?
   How can you remind yourself not to get too caught up in the trappings of success?

CHAPTER 47

The fascination of what's difficult

I once attended an aikido black belt grading test. As a lowly yellow belt, I was in awe of the students grading for black belt. It had taken them years of practice to prepare for this test, and to me they looked like the embodiment of fluency and mastery. But something Clive MacDonald, one of the examining *sensei*, said to them before the test has stayed with me:

"Your black belt is your first belt."

Of course, I knew that there were several grades (dans) of black belt. Having been thrown by first dans and a fourth dan, I can assure you there is a difference. But the sensei was suggesting something more radical: although we tend to think of a black belt as the ultimate achievement, we should treat it as a starting point, a marker of basic competence. The point at which learning begins.

When you are offered the job, or accepted onto the team, or certified, or published, or whatever, it can be tempting to feel like you've made it. But as any mountaineer knows, when you scale the highest peak you can see, another peak comes into view. If you're content to stop climbing, the only way is down.

If you're lucky, there will be the equivalent of a senior black belt around, to stop you slipping into the complacency and remind you how far you have to go. If you're unlucky, you'll be surrounded by yes-men—so you'll need to remind yourself.

Yeats wrote of "the fascination of what's difficult"—the drive to keep tackling the most challenging, inspiring, frustrating, and maddening challenges you can find. Whatever you achieve, whatever problem you solve, if you remain curious, you will always find another challenge that fascinates you. Rewards, honors, and the other trappings of success are nice to have, but nothing beats the challenge itself.

Some days this can feel dispiriting. "You mean I never get to put my feet up and rest on my laurels?" But more often than not, it's thrilling—it means you'll never exhaust the fascination of what's difficult, however long you live and however much you achieve.

YOUR NEXT STEPS

1. Remember a time you achieved something you never thought you could, that felt like an 'end point.'
    What happened afterwards?
    When and how did you encounter your next challenge?
    Was it something you set yourself, or did someone else challenge you?

2. Consider your current situation.
    Are you challenging yourself or resting on your laurels?
    If the latter, how can you rekindle the fascination of what's difficult?

NOTE

Sensei Clive MacDonald teaches aikido at Braintree Aiki Budo Kai: www.babk.org.uk

CHAPTER 48

Leap before you look

Remember Kiyomizu-dera?

When you pass through the gate and enter the temple, you come to a large wooden platform overlooking a steep drop. From below, you can hear the sound of a waterfall that is reputed to grant the wishes of those who drink its waters.

In Japan, the phrase 'to leap off the platform at Kiyomizu-dera' means to take a leap of faith, committing yourself to a decision or course of action, even though there are no guarantees of success. The saying harks back to the Edo period, when people leapt off the wooden platform for real—the idea was that if you could survive the 40-foot drop, your wish would be granted.

These days, nobody actually jumps off the platform anymore. But the Japanese say that at some point in everyone's life, they have to leap off the platform at Kiyomizu-dera. Sooner or later, you will be faced with a decision—about love, your career, your business, or something else—where you have to decide whether or not to take a leap of faith, with no guarantees, and no obvious means of support. Maybe you'll land in a heap. Maybe you'll have a soft landing. Or maybe you'll fly...

When I first heard this, I had to laugh. Looking back on my own life and career, it felt like I'd jumped off the platform at least a dozen times! I had been constantly trying new things, launching new projects, and trying to make them work in mid-air. I'd crashed to earth plenty of times, experiencing rejection, criticism, and plain unvarnished failure. I'd also had the satisfaction of landing on my feet and having my wish granted. And once or twice, I'd experienced flight.

Whatever the result, when I look back at all the leaps I've made, it's hard for me to regret any of them. Sometimes the lessons they taught me were painful—but there was always a lesson, if I paid attention. And each time I tasted success, it made the failures and disappointments worthwhile.

Last time I visited Kyomizu-dera was the day before my wedding, in brilliant January sunshine. Another leap I'm glad I made.

I can also think of a few times where I was faced with a leap but didn't have the courage. Those missed chances I do regret—because I'll never know what would have happened if I had seized them.

One day, maybe very soon, you will be faced with the prospect of a leap from your own personal Kiyomizu-dera. You'll have to decide whether you're ready, and whether it's worth the risk. If you jump, there are no guarantees. But if you never leap, you're guaranteed regret.

You could spend the rest of your life wishing you had taken a leap of faith. Don't create that regret for yourself. And whatever you do, don't let the painted demons of Rejection and Criticism stop you pursuing your dream.

NOW WHAT?

CHAPTER 49

Time to get started

I showed the first draft of this book to several trusted advisors. They all came up with insightful and helpful suggestions for improving the book. And the one thing they all agreed on was they enjoyed the stories.

I hope you liked the stories too, and found some inspiration in them. That's why I encouraged you to read this book the first time without worrying too much about the 'next steps' sections.

But now you've got this far, I'd encourage you to stop and reflect on what you're going to do with the ideas in the book. Because I didn't write it *just* to entertain you—I wrote it to help you take action and make changes.

So here's what I suggest you do now:

1. Turn back to the Contents pages.
2. Read through the chapter titles and remember what each chapter was about.
3. Be alert for the 'emotional hotspots'—the twinges of fear, excitement, anger, or maybe just discomfort, that let you know which chapters have touched a nerve for you. Make a list of the 'hottest' chapters.
4. Now re-read those chapters, including the 'next steps' sections.
5. Pick one chapter and start working through the next steps— for real. Use my suggestions as a springboard for trying new things, and notice what results you get.

6. Don't be discouraged if you don't get instant results. If you get stuck down in one area, pick another chapter and see what progress you can make on another front. Like Rome, resilience isn't built in a day.

CHAPTER 50

Let me know how you get on...

I'd love to hear how you use the ideas in this book. You can let me know here: lateralaction.com/contact

If you'd like a free 26-week guide to taking a creative route to success... sign up for my course The Creative Pathfinder here: lateralaction.com/pathfinder

Or if you'd just like me to let you know when my next book comes out... join the advance notice list here: lateralaction.com/next-book

If you'd like me to help you with any of the challenges described in this book... I work with coaching clients all over the world via webcam, this page explains how: lateralaction.com/resilience-coaching

And if you found *Resilience* helpful... I'd be grateful if you would consider leaving a review (even a sentence or two) on Amazon. Not only will it help me, it will help other people like you to benefit from the ideas in the book.

Amazon US Amzn.to/13xcS2E

Amazon UK Amzn.to/16wKbWL

Thank you for reading this far, I hope you found the book helpful and I wish you success and fulfillment on your journey.

Mark McGuinness

278

Acknowledgments

Thank you to the following people who helped to make *Resilience* a better book:

Gary Smailes, my editor, for insightful and helpful suggestions.

Irene Hoffman Design, for a radiant cover design and impeccable typography.

Jarie Bolander, Quentin S. Crisp, John Eaton, and Christina Saunders, for valuable feedback on the original draft.

Sarah Ridley, for proofreading the book and picking up lots of things I'd missed.

My coaching clients, blog readers, and the Creative Pathfinders, for teaching me what's important to you.

Scott Belsky, Jocelyn Glei, Sean Blanda, and the rest of the Behance team, for letting me road-test some of these ideas with the creative community at 99u.com

Steven Pressfield, for inspiration and encouragement.

Catherine Kirk, John Eaton, Ray Keedy-Lilley, Pamela Gawler-Wright, and Roy Johnson, for teaching me about feedback, transformation and building resilience.

The teachers at Amaravati Buddhist Monastery, for showing me what mindfulness means.

Sue Dove, Geoff Reilly, Mimi Khalvati, Brian Clark, Naomi Dunford and Dave Navarro, for teaching me different aspects of the writer's craft.

Sensei Tony Ecclestone and all at Meridian Aikido, for showing me how to fall over properly (and get back up again).

My parents, long-term sources of resilience.

Last but not least, my wife Mami, who believed in the project from the start.

About the Author

Mark McGuinness is a writer and coach who has been helping people achieve remarkable things since 1996.

Based in the UK, his blog at LateralAction.com is read by thousands of people every week, and he coaches clients all over the world via the magic of the internet. He is a co-author of the book *Manage Your Day-to-Day: Build Your Routine, Find Your Focus and Sharpen Your Creative Mind*, and the author of a series of popular ebooks, including *Time Management for Creative People*, downloaded over 100,000 times. Mark's work as an agent of change has been featured in publications including *Creative Review* and the *Wall Street Journal*, and in a TV documentary for the Discovery Health Channel.

He holds a BA in English Language & Literature from Oxford University and an MA in Creative & Media Enterprises from the University of Warwick. He is a psychotherapist registered with the UK Council for Psychotherapy (UKCP).

Mark's own creative medium is poetry—he writes about classic and contemporary poetry at MarkMcGuinness.com

In between writing and client sessions, he shares bite-sized inspiration online:

Twitter.com/markmcguinness
Facebook.com/lateralaction
Gplus.to/markmcguinness